SIMPLY BENTO

DELICIOUS BOX LUNCH IDEAS FOR
HEALTHY PORTIONS TO GO

YUKO and NORIKO,
creators of *Japanese Cooking 101*

Race Point
PUBLISHING

Brimming with creative inspiration, how-to projects, and useful information to enrich your everyday life, Quarto Knows is a favorite destination for those pursuing their interests and passions. Visit our site and dig deeper with our books into your area of interest: Quarto Creates, Quarto Cooks, Quarto Homes, Quarto Lives, Quarto Drives, Quarto Explores, Quarto Gifts, or Quarto Kids.

First published in 2018 by Race Point,
an imprint of The Quarto Group,
142 West 36th Street, 4th Floor,
New York, NY 10018, USA
T (212) 779-4972 F (212) 779-6058
www.QuartoKnows.com

Race Point titles are also available at discount for retail, wholesale, promotional, and bulk purchase. For details, contact the Special Sales Manager by email at specialsales@quarto.com or by mail at The Quarto Group, Attn: Special Sales Manager, 401 Second Avenue North, Suite 310, Minneapolis, MN 55401, USA.

10 9 8 7 6 5 4 3 2 1

ISBN: 978-1-63106-510-1

Editorial Director: Jeannine Dillon
Managing and Project Editor: Erin Canning
Photographer: Anett Velsberg-Tiedemann

Printed in China

CONTENTS

WHAT IS BENTO?

Bento, written as **弁当** in Japanese, is a packed meal that is commonly eaten as lunch in Japan. Many school children and workers take a single-portion, homemade meal packed in a bento box to school or to the office every day. Bento is also a popular take-out food, sold pretty much everywhere you go in Japan, from convenience stores and train stations to high-end department store delis. Many traditional restaurants serve bento only during lunchtime—often in a wood or lacquered bento box—or you can sample beautifully prepared dishes from an elaborate multicourse meal in one simple box at a much lower price.

Bento culture has such a long and diverse history in Japan that it is hard to define exactly why people eat bento. The oldest records show that people were already eating portable, dried rice as early as the fifth century. When the tea ceremony culture developed, elaborate lacquer wares, which held food—similar to today's bento boxes—started to appear. By the 1600s, the upper class were bringing along these lacquer wares so they could eat while enjoying cherry-blossom viewing parties. Ever since then, bento has been a part of Japanese culture. People ate *makunouchi bento*, an upscale mixed bento, at the intermissions of plays in the Edo period (1603–1867). Lower-ranked samurai, who made less money, brought their own bento lunches to work to save money, just like Japanese "salary men" today. In the late nineteenth century, when people started traveling by train, *ekiben*, the bento sold at train stations ("eki"), started to become popular. There are hundreds of ekiben all over the country today for people traveling on the many trains in Japan.

BENTO FOR EVERYONE

Bento has become so popular that if there is a demand from anybody, there is a kind of bento available. The "hot" bento chain stores started to spread throughout the country during the 1980s, and people ate those freshly made bentos as meals at home for dinner, not just for lunch. Convenience stores began to carry varieties of reasonably priced bento, and they became popular among students and young singles who did not want to cook. *Depachika*, the underground gourmet food floor found in department stores, attracted housewives for fancy bento to bring home, to have a break from daily cooking. *Kyaraben*, or character bento, incorporates cute characters from animation or other pop culture into the bento food. For example, a mother might make the face of a child's favorite TV character by carefully arranging rice and vegetables. They first became popular among mothers of small children, and it has continued to inspire people on social media. Today kyaraben is a big industry, selling all kinds of tools and products for making these cute and amusing bento.

Many people, however, use bento for pragmatic reasons, such as people who bring their own lunches to school or work, where food is not readily available; even people who have access to cafeterias and restaurants make and bring bento. The reasons may vary—whether it's economic, convenience, health or safety, or simply that they prefer bento meals.

In recent years, bento has become increasingly popular outside of Japan. We have started to see more food establishments serving bento, and there are more blogs, articles, and books about bento, many of them are written in English. Many bento enthusiasts around the world proudly post their neatly prepared bento photos on social media, and you can buy all kinds of bento boxes, accessories, and tools from online stores. The trending bentos are not necessarily the traditional Japanese versions, and range from quick and easy food to elaborate kyaraben.

THE BENEFITS OF BENTO

What motivates us to make bento is that it enables us to make safe and healthy lunches for our families. Like most parents, we don't eat the same way we did when we were young and single. Watching what we put into our bodies—especially when feeding young children—seems more important than ever before. We want to feed our families with safe meals. We want to make sure they have enough nutrition. We know what is in the food. Beyond the food itself, we want to save money for our families' futures, to put away more for college and retirement funds, by not eating out all the time. But we are also busy with work and chores, and, yes, tired and lazy some days too! Bento makes it easy to get our kids the nutrition they need without using half the day to do it. We have become used to planning for bento as part of our everyday cooking. While making dinner, for example, we always make extra so there is enough for the next day's lunch, or we add a few extra steps, such as blanching and cutting vegetables the night before for a bento lunch the next day. We'll share these tips and tricks throughout the book with you.

Not sure if you can successfully incorporate bento into your busy life? We have an ultimate form of bento in Japan called *osechi*, which is the New Year feast. Osechi consists of layered boxes filled with many small dishes, and there are many tedious steps for making each dish. The work of making all the osechi dishes is so overwhelming that these days, more people are buying this feast rather than preparing it themselves. So how do you preserve a rich tradition such as osechi without the hours of tedious steps? The secret is that you really don't have to make it *perfectly*. We once read in a cooking magazine that you can learn to make osechi by preparing only one homemade dish and then buying the rest of the dishes elsewhere. That same idea can apply for daily bento-making too. If a bento recipe seems like too much work, start with one of our 10-Minute Bento (page 87) or try making just one Side Dish (page 163). Eventually, you'll feel comfortable enough to try two side dishes, and soon you'll be making complete bento meals in no time. Then one day, perhaps, you'll be skilled enough to prepare an osechi on your own!

THE STORY BEHIND JAPANESE COOKING 101

We met at our kids' preschool over ten years ago. While the kids were playing on the playground, we introduced ourselves and began to talk. We discovered that we were both originally from the Kansai region of Japan; Noriko grew up in Osaka, and Yuko in nearby Kyoto.

We moved to America in the early nineties and studied here. Noriko became a pastry chef while Yuko worked in software in Silicon Valley. We talked about kids, we talked about school, but mostly we talked about food. We are both avid home cooks and make Japanese food, American food, sweets, and, of course, bento at home. We realized that so many Americans liked Japanese food but found it intimidating to cook at home. We knew everyone could do it with some help, and so when our kids became older and we had a little more time to ourselves, we decided to make videos on how to make Japanese food at home with ease. This is how our website, Japanese Cooking 101 (japanesecooking101.com), was born. On the site, we try to show simpler ways of making your favorite Japanese foods with easy-to-find ingredients. We also introduce authentic dishes that Japanese families eat in their homes (besides sushi and tempura), so you can add a few new, delicious favorites to your dinner selections.

But we had another big ambition when we started our website: we wanted to pass the Japanese food culture on to our children. Our kids were born in America, and being second generation, they have not yet fully appreciated the wealth of their Japanese background. But we know that will likely change as they grow older and settle down with families of their own. Japanese food has always been an important part of the culture in our households, and the kids will miss it when we can't offer any it anymore. Hopefully, they will be able to enjoy the food they grew up with by using our recipes and then share it with their own families one day. We have also heard that many families with Japanese heritage have had trouble re-creating food from their childhoods and connecting to their history. So, if you have been unable to secure grandma's recipe for your favorite dish, we sincerely hope you find it at Japanese Cooking 101.

—Yuko and Noriko

INTRODUCTION TO SIMPLY BENTO

Making bento is something we've been doing almost every day since our kids started attending school. And just like every busy parent out there, we don't want to spend our whole day making bento. We plan and prepare for bento to save both time and money. We use leftovers. We use convenient products like precut vegetables. We prep at night so that we can pack and go in the morning.

Bento-making was sometimes something of a mundane chore for us until Jeannine Dillon at Race Point Publishing contacted us about creating a *Simply Bento* cookbook. Starting this project made us think more of what bento means to us. Let's face it, making bento will always be more work than premade lunches from the store or throwing a sandwich in a bag, so why do we still make bento the way we do? The answer is simple: it is about our families' well-being. We want them to be healthy and happy. We want to avoid preservatives and ingredients we can't pronounce. There is a great American saying, "you are what you eat"; this concept is connected to the idea of bento. By choosing, making, and putting good food in bento, it's better for our families. It is okay not to make everything in bento from scratch, or not even every day. A bento is not just food in a box; it is also the thought and care from the person making the bento. A busy kid may not notice this every day, but it will stay with them over the years, as it did with us. We even find ourselves copying the things our own mothers did in our bentos!

In this book, we show you how to make the classic and popular bentos from Japan, as well as not-so-traditional bentos that we like and think everyone would enjoy no matter where you live. Many of our Japanese recipes are just as authentic as how our moms prepared them, but we have simplified some parts, both ingredients and steps, to make them more suited to bento and easier to make.

We believe that what goes into bento should not be any different from what we would normally eat at home. Having lived in two countries, Japan and the United States, we have a range of comfort food. We certainly love the traditional Japanese food that our moms made, such as teriyaki, simmered vegetables, and grilled fish, but we also have a lot more food that we regularly cook at home for our family—from pasta and tacos to roast beef.

Many of our recipes are customizable to suit your dietary needs. We have a dedicated chapter for low-carb and vegan, but you can also use any bento recipe in the book and customize it by replacing carbohydrates with more vegetables, meats, or plant-based proteins.

HOW TO MAKE BENTO: 7 KEY POINTS

Whether you are already packing lunches or thinking about starting soon, the idea of making bento every morning can be both exciting and daunting. You may not know where to begin or realize how easy it can be to make bento that you and your family will enjoy. Here are the 7 Key Points for making bento a reality, including important safety tips, what food to pack, how to select bento boxes, and putting it all together.

1. SAFETY FIRST

Bento is usually eaten at room temperature, unless you have access to a microwave or hot food is packed in a thermal container. However, from the time you pack the food in the morning to the time it is eaten at school or work, bacteria can grow inside of a bento box. It is very important to pay attention to the following food safety rules to keep everyone safe.

- Keep everything clean, including your hands and utensils. Avoid cross contamination by switching utensils when cooking raw meat and packing cooked dishes. Use a dishwasher, if you can, or hot soapy water to clean bento boxes well after each and every use.
- All foods must be thoroughly cooked unless they are meant to be eaten raw. No sashimi, runny eggs, or medium-rare steak for bento unless you eat it right away at home.
- If you are packing leftovers, reheat them in the morning. Heating up leftovers in a toaster or conventional oven or microwave will freshen the food and kill bacteria.
- Cool food completely before closing the lid. Imagine steamy rice straight from the rice cooker warming up the temperature inside the box, which could become a breeding ground for bacteria.
- Keep hot food hot and cold food cold. Packing a bento box in an insulated bag with an ice pack will help maintain the freshness of cold food; use a thermal container for hot food. You want to avoid the temperatures between 40°F to 140°F (4°C to 60°C), known as the "Danger Zone" according to the United States Department of Agriculture.
- Try adding natural antibiotics. It's been said that some foods, such as salt, vinegar, and ginger, help suppress bacteria and prevent bento from spoiling. This is one of the reasons why many bento dishes include vegetable sides that are well-seasoned or marinated in vinegar. Umeboshi (pickled sour plums; page 16) are believed to be the best of all and are often used as a filling for Onigiri (rice balls; page 165) rice balls or a topping for Steamed Rice (page 18).

2. AIM FOR A BALANCED DIET

One of the main purposes for making bento in the first place is to provide a healthy meal for your family or yourself when outside of the home. So, if you are reading this book, you are more likely health conscious and already seeking a balanced diet; however, you do not need to be super picky or stressed out about adding all the nutrients you need for a day in a bento box. A good rule of thumb for packing a reasonably healthy bento is to include a main dish rich in protein along with a carbohydrate and a couple of vegetable sides and/or fruits. (Read more about Bento Ingredients on page 17.)

3. PACK WHAT YOU LIKE TO EAT

Although bento originated in Japan, today's bento ingredients are not limited to Japanese food. In fact, you should pack the kind of food that you and your family *like* to eat. If you enjoy Mexican food, for example, pack a cut-up quesadilla with salad. If soup is your thing, whip up a quick vegetable soup and pack it in a thermal jar. If you are following a special diet, pack what you can eat. What goes inside the bento box should not be much different from what you would normally eat at home. You can be adventurous and try something new, of course, but try it out for dinner first, just in case you don't like it and there is no other option for lunch.

4. PLAN AHEAD

You may have seen bentos made by other people and wondered how they can pack so many different dishes in a bento each and every day. The truth is that many bentos we make are with leftovers from the night before. Add a few side dishes made ahead of time or quickly prepared in the morning in the box, and you will have a typical and decent-looking bento. With a little bit of planning the day before or during the weekend, bento-making becomes so much easier and realistic. The majority of our featured recipes are great served as a main dish for dinner. Since the recipes in this book are for 2 servings (except for the Bento at Home chapter, on page 151), it is easy to double or triple the recipes in order to make enough portions for dinner and bento. You will find Plan Ahead snippets throughout this book to help you plan better.

5. CHOOSE THE RIGHT BENTO BOX

While there are many different types of containers that you can use for bento (see Bento Boxes and Accessories on page 12), you should choose the right kind depending on the type of food you pack. For example, a large box with compartments is great for sandwiches and cut-up fruits, while a more compact Japanese-style bento box is easier to fill for a classic bento with rice and a few small dishes. A deeper container is ideal for noodles and rice bowls. We recommend you keep a few boxes of different sizes and depths, and choose depending on the kind of bento you're packing.

6. PACK ATTRACTIVELY

Assembling a bento box is like plating a dinner. You can certainly pack what's left from the night before, "as is," without much thought and call it a bento. However, you don't need to be a bento artist to make a more attractive bento. Follow the few tips below, and you can pack a bento with ease and make it look appealing. An added bonus is that good-looking bentos tend to be healthier too!

- Start packing with larger dishes. We find it easier to start with something that takes up more space, such as rice followed by a main dish and sides. You want to think about which direction to pack, depending on the size of the dish. For example, if the teriyaki fish you are packing as a main dish takes up the whole length of the bento box, pack some rice diagonally on one side and place the fish on the edge of the rice. Fill the other half with a few side dishes.

- Compartmentalize. You can use the built-in dividers in a bento box or insert baking cups (page 12) to easily compartmentalize. Or even better, some healthy edibles, such as green leaf lettuce or shiso leaves, can be used to separate one food from another.
- Pack tightly with no space. The difference between a dinner plate and a bento is that a plate sits still on a table while a bento is moved around, sometimes completely upside down in a kid's backpack. If there is a lot of space left in the box, use small vegetables, such as grape tomatoes, baby carrots, and snap peas, to fill the small gaps.
- Add contrasting colors. Preparing a colorful bento with contrasting colors makes a bento not only more attractive but also healthier. Carbs and meat tend to be brown and white, so be sure to add a rainbow of colors in a bento by packing a variety of vegetables and fruits. (Read more about Vegetables on page 23.)

7. MAKE IT A ROUTINE

Still too much of a hassle to make bento? Try establishing a routine that works best for you. For example, first thing in the morning, open the rice cooker and place the rice in the bento box and let it start cooling. Then, place leftovers saved from the night before in a toaster or conventional oven to reheat. So far, it has only taken a few minutes. Now you can start brewing your coffee (a must!) and prepare breakfast while working on a couple of quick and easy bento sides. Some side dishes, such as vegetable sticks and salad, are great served for breakfast too! Place everything in a bento box without the lid on and let all the components cool completely while you get ready or enjoy breakfast with your cup of coffee. All you have left to do is to close the lid!

BENTO ESSENTIALS

BENTO BOXES AND ACCESSORIES

There are a large variety of containers that you can use for bento, from traditional bentwood boxes, handcrafted in Japan, to simple food-storage containers. Common materials for bento boxes are plastic, stainless steel, ceramic, or wood. There is no one perfect bento box for everything; in fact, we tend to have several favorite containers that we use often and switch around depending on the type of food to be packed. Here are some tips for selecting bento boxes and convenient accessories that make bento-making easier and fun.

BENTO BOXES

FOOD-STORAGE CONTAINERS
You can use any kind of food-safe containers to pack bento, in all sizes, shapes, and materials. Large, shallow rectangular boxes are handy for packing sandwiches, while deeper round containers are great for salads, noodles, and rice bowls.

BENTO BOXES WITH DIVIDERS AND/OR COMPARTMENTS
When packing a classic bento with a main dish and a few sides, a bento box with a divider or compartments is easier to use. A compartmentalized bento box helps you pack a variety of food besides a main dish, including fruits and vegetables. They are also great for portion control.

TIERED OR STACKABLE BOXES
Stackable boxes are convenient when there are different types of food that you don't want to mix, such as rice and sauce or sandwiches and salad. Some people prefer stackable containers to boxes with compartments because they tend to be smaller in size and can fit in a corner of a bag or backpack.

INSULATED THERMAL FOOD JARS
Insulated food jars keep food warm or cold for hours; hence, these are great for packing soups, stews, and yogurt. Since they are sealed well, they are leakproof.

WOODEN BOXES
Traditional handcrafted wooden bento boxes have gained popularity in recent years, despite the price tag (some can be over $80!). They are not dishwasher or microwave safe, and they are not leakproof. However, bento presented in handcrafted wooden boxes are so pretty, and they say rice packed in an uncoated wooden box becomes better tasting as the natural wood absorbs excess moisture.

LACQUER BOXES (*JUBAKO*)
These boxes are used for bento to be eaten at home or served at restaurants. They are typically coated in black and red lacquer, and some have fixed or removable dividers.

DISPOSABLE CONTAINERS
Disposable or compostable food containers that are used as "to-go" boxes from restaurants can be convenient when you simply want to discard the box after you are done eating. These are great for traveling or sharing with others.

ACCESSORIES

BAKING CUPS AND DIVIDERS
There are a number of different ways to divide and separate food, even in the simplest containers. Silicone or aluminum baking cups or paper cups made especially for bento are essentials to help compartmentalize your bento box. They come in many bright colors and different shapes. Grass-shaped plastic food separators called *baran* (often found on sushi platters) are also used to add a barrier between dishes that have different flavors.

BENTO UTENSILS
Utensils with plastic cases are convenient for carrying clean or used utensils. Some bento boxes have a utensil case built in the lid.

CONDIMENT CONTAINERS
Small containers with tight lids are convenient for carrying condiments, dipping sauces, and salad dressing. Just make sure they are leakproof

FOOD PICKS
There are many cute food picks available, with characters or charms on one end, which will transform an ordinary lunch into a fun and decorative bento. They are also great for holding food together and making it easy for older children to pick up finger food.

FOOD MOLDS
Use egg molds to shape hard-boiled eggs into your favorite animal or shape. If you are not good at making Onigiri (rice balls; page 165), you can use a rice ball mold to make evenly shaped onigiri.

VEGETABLE AND COOKIE CUTTERS
Small, stainless-steel vegetable cutters are used to make flower-shaped carrots that you often see in a classic Japanese dish. Cookie cutters are great for cutting sandwiches into fun shapes.

ICE PACKS
Reusable ice packs are a must-have for keeping food fresh and safe.

JAPANESE PANTRY ESSENTIALS

Although Japanese cooking is not as difficult as some may think, you should have a few basic ingredients on hand in your pantry to make authentic Japanese dishes. We try to use ingredients that are easily accessible, but some of the them may not be familiar to you. Crucial items, such as seasonings, are mostly readily available at many local supermarkets, but others are found only at Japanese and Asian markets or online. You don't need to acquire everything right away. Start with the first items on the list and gradually add more items as you challenge yourself with new dishes.

SOY SAUCE

Soy sauce, or *shoyu* (/shoh-yu/), a Japanese staple seasoning, is a dark-brown liquid made from soybeans. It is quite salty, but it has a caramelized aroma and more flavorful taste than mere salt. It gives dishes a distinct flavor and darker color. Widely used commercial soy sauce often includes wheat. If you follow a gluten-free diet, choose gluten-free soy sauce or tamari soy sauce, which doesn't use any wheat products (or very little). It is available in almost any grocery store.

SAKE

Sake (/sah-kay/) is Japanese rice wine and an essential ingredient for Japanese cooking. When it is used for cooking, it tenderizes meat, cuts odors (such as fish smell), and gives deeper flavor to dishes. It may be found at grocery stores in a liquor aisle or Asian ingredients aisle or at liquor stores. If Japanese markets are available near you, you might be able to find cooking sake (*ryourishu*) too. If you have limited alcohol intake, you can just omit it.

MIRIN

Mirin (/mee-rin/) is sweet rice wine widely used in Japanese cooking. Mirin is made from steamed *mochi* rice and malted rice that are fermented with added alcohol. In the process of fermentation, the rice produces a lot of sugar along with alcohol, which turns out very

sweet. Mirin gives food sweetness, shine, and a good aroma. It is used like cooking sake, but it has a much sweeter taste, which is perfect for some Japanese dishes. If you have limited alcohol intake, you can substitute mirin with sugar and water (1:3 ratio) or a smaller amount of sweetener, such as honey or agave syrup.

MISO PASTE

Miso (/mee-soh/) paste is a paste made from fermented soybeans and used to season soups, sauces, and other dishes. It is quite salty but flavorful, and a staple seasoning in Japanese cooking. White miso has a sweeter and milder flavor, while red miso has a saltier and more mature taste. White miso is preferred in the Kyoto region in western Japan, and red is more popular in central Japan. The most popular and versatile type of miso is mixed miso (*awase miso*). It falls somewhere between white and red miso. Typical miso soup is made with this mixed miso. Some markets carry miso in the Asian food or refrigerated section; otherwise, it can be found at Japanese markets, Asian markets, or online.

RICE VINEGAR

Rice vinegar, or *su* (/su/), is made from fermented rice. Japanese rice vinegar is a yellowish clear color, and it has a milder and more neutral flavor than other vinegars. It is used in many Japanese foods, such as sushi and pickled vegetables. Rice vinegar can be found at a lot of supermarkets or you can buy it online.

OILS

Oils used in Japanese cooking are mostly vegetable oils that have neutral flavors, such as canola or corn oil. Sesame oil has a very strong aroma and flavor and is used sporadically to flavor salads and other dishes. *Rayu* is chili pepper–infused sesame oil that is often used in sauces for Chinese-style dishes, such as gyoza dumplings. Feel free to use any vegetable oil you prefer, as there are many options available today.

KATSUOBUSHI (DRIED BONITO) FLAKES

Bonito is a kind of tuna, and *katsuobushi* (/kah-tsu-oh-bu-shee/) is dried, smoked bonito. Katsuobushi are flakes shaved from a piece of dried fish. This is actually called *kezuribushi*, but it is also known as katsuobushi. A lot of readily available katsuobushi is only smoked and dried, but the more traditional katsuobushi is smoked and then ripened with a special kind of mold for months to a couple years. Katsuobushi is usually sold as flakes or shavings in a package, but you can buy a chunk of dried fish and shave it yourself with a katsuobushi plane if you would like to make your own. Katsuobushi has a smoky, savory fragrance and taste that is a great accent for many Japanese dishes. Because dried bonito is packed with a lot of umami (savory taste), it is perfect for making Dashi (fish broth; page 20), which is a crucial component in Japanese cooking. Katsuobushi also can be used by itself, sprinkled on simple vegetables to instantly give a deeper flavor.

KOMBU (DRIED KELP)

Kombu (/kohm-bu/), or *konbu*, is dried, edible sea kelp that is mainly used to make Dashi (fish broth; page 20) in Japanese cooking. It has a subtle yet great savory taste (umami), when it is boiled in water. Kombu should be rehydrated in cool water and then cooked to extract its umami flavor. Kombu Dashi (page 21) is a perfect broth for vegetarians because it is plant-based. When kombu is rehydrated, it grows about three times in size and becomes a soft, tasty ingredient for many dishes, such as *nimono* (simmered dish) and *tsukudani* (strongly flavored kombu).

DRIED SHIITAKE MUSHROOMS

Dried shiitake (/shee-tah-kay/) mushrooms are used in many *nimono* (simmered dish) recipes in Japan. Dried shiitake have a stronger flavor than fresh shiitake mushrooms. They need to be rehydrated in water before use; the flavorful liquid from the rehydration can be used as broth in some recipes.

TOGARASHI

Togarashi (/toh-gah-rah-shee/) are Japanese dried red chile peppers that are similar to peppers found in Mexican cuisine. When the chile pod is used in cooking, the seeds are removed and the pods are thinly sliced. Only a small amount is used to accent dishes. *Shichimi togarashi* (also called *nanami togarashi*) is a spicy powder that is often sprinkled on hot noodle soups. Shichimi is a mixture of togarashi powder and other ingredients, such as orange peel, white and black sesame seeds, Japanese pepper (*sanshou*), ginger, and green seaweed.

WASABI

Wasabi (/wah-sah-bee/) is a kind of Japanese horseradish which is usually grated and used for various Japanese dishes. It is spicy and known because of sushi. It is hard to find fresh wasabi outside of Japan, but it is widely available in a paste form in tubes at most supermarkets. Wasabi can be very hot, but it is more like the power of Western horseradish than chile pepper. It can have a strong effect in your nose.

NORI (ROASTED SEAWEED)

Roasted seaweed is called *sushi nori* (/su-shee noh-ree/), or *yaki nori* (/yah-kee noh-ree/), in Japanese. It is used for rolled sushi. Roasted seaweed has a mild but distinctive seafood flavor. It is thin and crisp on its own, but becomes somewhat chewy when it absorbs moisture from rice. Roasted seaweed is seaweed that has been dried and roasted, and then made into a papery form, perfect for holding rice and fillings. Roasted seaweed for making sushi is usually sold in 8-inch (20 cm) squares. The sheet has a front side and a back side; the shiny side is the front side, which should be on the outside of sushi rolls. You may find smaller squares or rectangular seaweed, *ajitsuke nori*, which is already seasoned. This can work well with food using regular rice, such as Onigiri (rice balls; page 165). There is also the convenient, already-shredded *kizami nori*, which can be used as a topping for various rice dishes.

WAKAME (SEAWEED)

Wakame (/wah-kah-meh/) is seaweed that is often found in dried form as opposed to seaweed that is fresh and salt preserved. Rehydrate it in water for 10 minutes, and it is ready to use. It expands to ten times the size of the dried pieces. Wakame has a mild flavor and soft texture, and is commonly used in soups and salads.

TONKATSU SAUCE

Tonkatsu (/tohn-kah-tsu/) sauce is a thick brown sauce made with Worcestershire sauce and used mainly for topping Tonkatsu (deep-fried pork; page 42). It can be used for the base seasoning in other dishes, such as Yakisoba (stir-fried noodles; page 94) and Okonomiyaki (savory cabbage pancake; page 79). Japanese Worcestershire sauce contains more fruits and vegetables, such as tomatoes and apples, than its Western counterpart. Tonkatsu sauce has a similar flavor to Japanese Worcestershire sauce, but its texture is thicker.

UMEBOSHI (PICKLED SOUR PLUM)

Umeboshi (/u-meh-boh-shee/) is pickled sour plum and has been eaten for over a thousand years in Japan. Ripened plums are marinated with salt and then sun-dried and preserved for a couple months to develop the flavor. Red perilla leaves (*shiso*) are pickled along with the plums to give a nice red color. It tastes salty and sour, and goes well with rice. It can be used whole (with or without a pit) to put in Onigiri (rice balls; page 165) as a filling. Umeboshi is said to suppress bacteria, and is often is used in bento lunches for this reason, because the bento may be kept at room temperature for a couple hours. It can also be chopped up and added to sauces or other dishes as a flavoring.

BENISHOGA (PICKLED RED GINGER)

Pickled red ginger, or *benishoga* (/beh-nee-shoh-gah/), is ginger pickled in plum vinegar. It is bright red and has a sour flavor with a little gingery spiciness. It is used in various dishes, such as Okonomiyaki (savory cabbage pancake; page 79) and Yakisoba (stir-fried noodles; page 94), and also is a great accompaniment for rice bowl dishes. It is tasty on its own, but it is also a nice garnish for its color. (Note that benishoga is not the same thing as sushi ginger.)

SESAME SEEDS

Sesame seeds, or *goma*—both white and black—are often used in Japanese dishes. Most of the time, they are toasted to make them more fragrant rather than being used raw. To make the flavor even stronger, seeds are ground in a mortar and pestle or a mill. Sesame seeds are also used to garnish rice and vegetables.

BENTO INGREDIENTS

CARBOHYDRATES

STEAMED RICE

Japanese bento traditionally contains steamed rice as its main carbohydrate. Japanese rice is a short-grain rice which is soft and sticky. It is easily picked up in bunches by chopsticks and also can be molded into various shapes. Japanese short-grain rice can be found in the Asian food section of most grocery stores.

Steamed rice is typically packed on one side of a bento box and side dishes on the other side. There is no need to season the rice; however, it is often garnished with *furikake* (seasoning; page 24) or Umeboshi (pickled sour plum; opposite). Onigiri (rice balls; page 165) is a popular rice dish in bento. It is often shaped into a triangle or a cylinder and stuffed with various fillings and wrapped with Nori (roasted seaweed; opposite). It is an easy and convenient food that can be eaten by hand for a quick bite. Sushi rolls are also a frequent pick for bento lunches. It is important to note that the sushi roll filling should not be traditional raw fish like at a restaurant, because the sushi roll in a bento is often kept at room temperature for hours and raw fish would be unsafe; cooked vegetables and eggs are more suitable.

You may swap Steamed Brown Rice (page 19) for Steamed White Rice (page 18) for any of the recipes in this book. Some brands of brown rice might be harder to mold into shapes because it may be less sticky than white rice. You may want to experiment with different kinds of brown rice to find what suits your taste and recipes.

BREAD

In Japan, sandwiches are a popular lunch option. Japanese sandwich bread is called *shoku pan*, and the thickness of the bread slices varies. Thinner slices (½ inch, or 13 mm, thick) are more suitable for sandwiches. If you cannot find shoku pan, simply substitute with bread of your choice, be it white or wheat, rolls or buns, or whatever your preference.

NOODLES

Noodles are a great carbohydrate for bento, especially for dishes that require dipping sauce or broth—it is easy to pack any liquid in a separate leakproof container. This way you can enjoy a dish that tastes freshly made instead of a soggy one sitting in a sauce or broth for hours.

STEAMED WHITE RICE

If you are using an electric rice cooker:

PREP TIME: 5 MINUTES   **COOK TIME:** 50 MINUTES   **YIELD:** 4 SERVINGS

2 cups (12 ounces, or 340 g) short-grain white rice (using the 6 ounces, or 180 ml, cup that comes with the rice cooker)

1 Place the rice in a bowl. Wash the rice and pour the water out. Repeat this process 2 more times.

2 Place the washed rice in the bowl of the rice cooker. Add enough water to reach the line for 2 cups of rice.

3 Cook according to the rice cooker instructions.

If you are using a stovetop:

PREP TIME: 5 MINUTES (PLUS 30 MINUTES SOAKING)   **COOK TIME:** 30 MINUTES   **YIELD:** 2 SERVINGS

1 cup (190 g) short-grain white rice
1½ cups (350 ml) water

1 Place the rice in a bowl. Wash the rice and pour the water out. Repeat this process 2 more times.

2 Place the washed rice and the 1½ cups (350 ml) water in a heavy-bottomed pot with a lid. Let the rice soak for 30 minutes.

3 Heat the pot, uncovered, over high heat until the water comes to a boil. Stir and reduce the heat to low. Cover the rice and cook for 15 minutes.

4 Remove the pot from the heat and let it stand, covered, for 10 minutes.

STEAMED BROWN RICE

If you are using an electric rice cooker:

PREP TIME: 5 MINUTES   **COOK TIME:** 1 HOUR 30 MINUTES (DEPENDING ON THE RICE COOKER)
YIELD: 4 SERVINGS

2 cups (12 ounces, or 340 g)
   brown rice (*genmai*; using
   the 6-ounce or, 180 ml, cup
   that comes with the rice
   cooker)

1 Place the rice in a bowl. Wash the rice and pour the water out. Repeat this process 2 more times.

2 Place the washed rice in the bowl of the rice cooker. Add enough water to the rice to reach the line for 2 cups of brown rice.

3 Cook according to the rice cooker instructions.

If you are using a stovetop:

PREP TIME: 5 MINUTES (PLUS 1 HOUR SOAKING)   **COOK TIME:** 40 MINUTES   **YIELD:** 2 SERVINGS

1 cup (190 g) brown rice
   (*genmai*)
2 cups (475 ml) water

1 Put the rice in a bowl. Wash the rice and pour the water out. Repeat this process 2 more times.

2 Place the washed rice and the 2 cups (475 ml) water in a heavy-bottomed pot with a lid. Let the rice soak for about 1 hour.

3 Heat the pot, uncovered, over high heat until the water comes to a boil. Stir and reduce the heat to low. Cover the rice and cook for 25 to 30 minutes.

4 Remove the pot from the heat and let it stand, covered, for 10 minutes.

BROTH, SAUCES, AND DIPS

Having some useful broth, sauces, and dips in stock in your refrigerator or freezer will save time in the morning, make Japanese cooking much easier, and is a simple way to make your bento consistently delicious. While some sauces are too time consuming or next to impossible to make at home (e.g., soy sauce), some types of broth, sauces, and dips are quite easy to make with simple ingredients. The best part of making them at home is that you know exactly what goes into them (no bad stuff!).

DASHI

The key flavor of many Japanese dishes comes from umami, a savory or meaty taste that is considered one of the five basic tastes along with sweet, sour, bitter, and salty. *Dashi* is a flavorful basic broth packed with umami and typically made from Katsuobushi (dried bonito flakes; page 15), Kombu (dried kelp; page 15), or a combination of the two. It is an essential ingredient in Japanese cooking, especially for making soups and simmered vegetables. Packaged instant dashi granules are available and very popular both in and out of Japan, but depending on the brands, they contain unwanted ingredients, such as MSG. Here are some basic homemade dashi variations that can be used for any Japanese recipes that require dashi.

FEATURED RECIPE:

BASIC KATSUO DASHI (EASY AND VERSATILE)

COOK TIME: 5 MINUTES   **YIELD:** 4 CUPS (950 ML)

4 cups (950 ml) water
2 handfuls katsuobushi (dried bonito flakes)

1 In a medium pot, bring the water to a boil.

2 Add the katsuobushi, simmer for 2 to 3 minutes, and then strain.

KOMBU DASHI (VEGAN AND DELICATE FLAVOR)

PREP TIME: 30 MINUTES FOR SOAKING   **COOK TIME:** 5 MINUTES   **YIELD:** 4 CUPS (950 ML)

4 cups (950 ml) water
1 sheet (10 to 20 g) kombu
(dried sea kelp),
approximately 4 × 2 inches
(10 × 5 cm)

1 In a medium pot, add the water and soak the kombu for 30 minutes.

2 Heat over medium heat until just before boiling. Remove the kombu.

ICHIBAN DASHI

(COMBINATION OF KATSUO AND KOMBU; MOST FLAVORFUL)

COOK TIME: 10 MINUTES   **YIELD:** 4 CUPS (950 ML)

4 cups (950 ml) water
1 sheet (10 to 20 g)
kombu (dried sea kelp),
approximately 4 × 2 inches
(10 × 5 cm)
1 handful katsuobushi (dried
bonito flakes)

1 In a medium pot, add the water and kombu, and heat over medium until just before boiling. Remove the kombu.

2 Add the katsuobushi, bring the dashi to a boil, and then immediately turn off the heat. Set aside for 5 minutes, then strain.

PLAN AHEAD

Dashi should be refrigerated and used within 2 days, but it can last for 3 to 4 weeks in the freezer. Fill ice cube trays with dashi and freeze. Once frozen, transfer the dashi cubes to a freezer bag or a container with a lid.

PROTEINS

Adding one or two dishes high in protein in bento will help you and your family maintain their energy levels throughout the afternoon. You can include any type of protein in bento, both animal and plant-based. Chicken, beef, pork, seafood, and eggs are all common ingredients and great for main dishes, as long as they are thoroughly cooked (except in some recipes for Bento at Home on page 151). For vegetarian or vegan options, tofu, beans, nuts, and some vegetables, such as spinach, broccoli, and edamame, are all great choices for plant-based proteins.

FEATURED RECIPE:

TAMAGOYAKI

Tamagoyaki is one of the most classic and popular dishes you'll find in Japanese bentos. Thin layers of egg that are seasoned slightly sweet with mirin and soy sauce are rolled into a log shape and cut into pieces. Tamagoyaki is versatile and you can add various chopped vegetables and/or meat as mix-ins.

PREP TIME: 2 MINUTES   **COOK TIME:** 5 MINUTES   **YIELD:** 2 SERVINGS

4 eggs
1 tablespoon (15 ml) mirin
¼ teaspoon salt
¼ teaspoon soy sauce
1 teaspoon vegetable oil

TAMAGOYAKI VARIATIONS
In step 2, you can mix in one of the following ingredients to add flavor and color. If you add a lot of mix-ins, reduce the number of eggs to 3 and adjust the amount of salt.
- 3 green onions, chopped
- 2 slices ham, chopped
- ¼ cup (45 g) chopped cooked spinach
- 1 tablespoon (10 g) chopped benishoga (pickled red ginger), reduce salt to ⅛ teaspoon

1 In a medium bowl, combine all the ingredients, except the oil.

2 Heat a rectangular tamagoyaki pan or a small nonstick pan over medium-high heat and add the oil.

3 Pour a thin layer of egg mixture into the pan, tilting it to cover the bottom of the pan. After the egg has set a little, gently roll it into a log. (Start to roll when the bottom of the egg has set and there is still liquid on top.) With the egg roll at the edge of the pan, pour some more egg mixture to again cover the bottom of the pan. After the new layer has set, roll the log back onto the cooked thin egg and roll to the other end of the pan.

4 Repeat, adding egg to the pan and rolling it back and forth, until the egg mixture is used up.

5 Remove from the pan and cool for 3 to 4 minutes. Slice into ½-inch (13 mm) rounds.

VEGETABLES

Usually, there are two or three kinds of small side dishes besides the main dish and rice in bento. Because the entrée is often meat or fish, a lot of side dishes are vegetable dishes. They don't all have to be complicated dishes or recipes with many ingredients. One of the sides simply can be an uncooked item, an easy dish that only takes a few minutes to make, or leftovers from another meal.

COLOR

The kinds of vegetables for bento should be the same thing as you eat at home, but keep things colorful. The more color in the vegetables, often the more nutritional value in them. Think about the balance of colors when you build your bento. This rule may help when you make a meal plan for bento. For example, if you have beef for the main entrée (brown), then add Tamagoyaki (rolled eggs, yellow; page opposite), Spinach Ohitashi (salad, green; page 175), and a few cherry tomatoes (red). The vibrant colors will stimulate the appetite when the bento box is opened at lunchtime. You cannot underestimate how the colors of food influence your mood! Colorful foods help make you feel satisfied without weighing you down in the afternoon. Plus, you might get an added boost of happiness knowing someone took the time and thought to make this bento just for you.

THE BALANCE OF FLAVOR

The balance of flavor with a main entrée and the vegetable side dishes is important. The flavorings in each vegetable side dish should vary, so they don't taste the same. For example, if one vegetable dish is vinegary, you may want other dishes to be saltier or sweeter. This way, you are more likely to eat all the vegetables.

COOKING METHOD

In addition to balancing flavor, you should also try to vary the cooking method for the dishes in your bento. If your main entrée is deep-fried, for example, you may not want other dishes to be deep-fried too. When Chicken Karaage (fried chicken; page 74) is a main dish, you may want to pair it with less greasy side dishes, such as a fresh salad, Pickled Daikon Radish (page 200), and orange segments. Not only are there more vitamins and minerals that can be attained from those vegetables, but also, the fresh taste of salad and pickles will enhance the flavor of the hearty fried chicken. You can also consider the textures of the dishes and vary them. Variety is the spice of life, and it's true in a good bento too.

SUBSTITUTES

We used some Asian vegetables throughout the book, which some people may not be familiar with, such as baby bok choy and lotus root. If you are nervous to try a new vegetable or perhaps don't like those vegetables, you may want to swap Swiss chard for bok choy and potato for lotus root. You can always substitute with other vegetables, so don't feel as though you have to skip a recipe if you don't recognize a vegetable. Please improvise with any dish whenever you need or want to, to make things easier for your bento-making. Part of the art and fun of bento is using what you have on hand. You'll quickly get used to adjusting or substituting ingredients and recipes in ways that work well for your bento and family.

GARNISH

In Japanese culture, garnishing bento with ingredients of various colors is very important, as the garnish will help determine if your bento looks delicious. Color and arrangement play a big role in garnishing bento and can convey different feelings. For example, one bento could be very refined with subtle colors, reflecting the current season; another could be playful with bright colors and fun shapes; and yet a third could literally send a message with symbols, letters, or pictures in the garnishing itself.

VEGETABLES AND FRUITS

One way to add more color in bento without much work is using vegetables, such as cherry tomatoes and lettuce leaves. The bright red and green colors can instantly perk up a bento. Tomatoes are nutritious, so you will want to use them anyway. Lettuce not only gives your bento a nice green color, but it naturally works as a divider between dishes so that multiple flavors will not be mixed. Seasonal fruits are another way to add color and also work as a healthy dessert after lunch.

SEASONINGS

Garnishing with flavors and seasonings is also typical in bento. Steamed Rice (page 18) is often used in Japanese bento, and because the rice itself doesn't have very much taste, it is often sprinkled with furikake (rice seasoning) or Umeboshi (pickled sour plum; page 16). Not only do both of these things season the rice, but they also give a decorative look. Similarly, Sesame Seeds (page 16) and Katsuobushi (dried bonito flakes; page 15) are often used as a finishing touch on some vegetable side dishes.

SHAPES

Another way of garnishing bento is to make interesting shapes with the food itself. You can carve or use vegetable or cookie cutters (page 13) to cut vegetables or fruits (with leftover pieces from salads and soups). Heart- and star-shaped carrots and cucumbers in a bento will bring more fun to any kid's lunchtime. Use a food mold (page 13) to shape steamed rice into elegant flowers. Small vegetables or fruit can be skewered onto toothpicks or plastic picks (page 13) for older children and adults, giving another decorative, visual effect.

NON-EDIBLE GARNISH

Non-edible garnish, such as baking cups and dividers (page 13), also plays an important part of bento. You know that small plastic leaf or grass sheet that often comes with sushi? There are lots of other shapes and colors to use; they are practical and fun. There are cups with many colors and patterns on the market. You can buy these small knickknacks mainly online, although there are more places that carry bento-related accessories today.

NORITAMA FURIKAKE
(EGG AND ROASTED SEAWEED RICE SEASONING)

PREP TIME: 20 MINUTES   **COOK TIME:** 20 MINUTES   **YIELD:** ¼ CUP (ABOUT 12 SERVINGS OF 1 TEASPOON)

2 hard-boiled egg yolks

2 teaspoons sugar

¼ teaspoon salt

½ cup (6 g) packed katsuobushi (dried bonito flakes)

1 teaspoon soy sauce

2 teaspoons sesame seeds

2 teaspoons shredded nori (roasted seaweed), cut into small pieces

1 teaspoon aonori (dried green seaweed flakes)

1 Sieve the boiled yolks through a medium mesh strainer. In a small nonstick pan, combine the yolks, sugar, and salt, and cook over low heat until yolks become dry, 6 to 7 minutes. Stir often, taking care not to let the mixture burn. Set aside.

2 In another small nonstick pan over low heat, cook the katsuobushi (first crush it by hand) and soy sauce until dry, about 5 minutes, stirring often. Add the sesame seeds and cook another minute.

3 Transfer the mixture to a small bowl and stir in the seasoned yolks, nori, and aonori.

CLASSIC JAPANESE BENTO

Chicken Teriyaki Bento   **28**

Beef Roll-Up Bento   **31**

Tsukune Bento   **32**

Grilled Mackerel Bento   **33**

Beef Shigureni Bento   **34**

Sukiyaki Bento   **36**

Salmon Teriyaki Bento   **37**

Pork Shogayaki Bento   **38**

CHICKEN TERIYAKI BENTO

This chicken teriyaki can be quickly cooked in a frying pan. The shishito peppers are sautéed in the pan with the chicken toward the end of cooking, so a main dish and a side are prepared together. The authentic, homemade teriyaki sauce uses ingredients from the Japanese Pantry Essentials (page 14), so there is no need to buy the bottled version.

TO MAKE THIS BENTO

Each bento has a main-dish recipe (below), side-dish recipes (page 163), and additional ingredients.

Chicken Teriyaki with Shishito Peppers
  (see recipe below)
Steamed Rice (page 18), with furikake of choice

Cucumber and Radish Sunomono
  (page 199)
Seasonal fruits

PREP TIME: 1 MINUTE   **COOK TIME:** 12 MINUTES   **YIELD:** 2 SERVINGS

CHICKEN TERIYAKI WITH SHISHITO PEPPERS

1 tablespoon (15 ml) soy sauce
1 tablespoon (15 ml) sake
2 teaspoons sugar
1 teaspoon mirin
1 teaspoon vegetable oil
2 skinless, boneless chicken
  thighs
4 to 6 shishito peppers

1 In a small bowl, combine the soy sauce, sake, sugar, and mirin. Set aside.

2 Heat the oil in a frying pan over medium-high heat. Add the chicken and cook for 4 to 5 minutes. Flip the chicken, reduce the heat to medium, and continue cooking on the other side. Add the peppers to the same pan and cook and stir for 3 to 4 minutes.

3 When the chicken is cooked through, add the teriyaki sauce to the pan and cook until the sauce is reduced and the chicken is coated in the sauce.

4 Cut the cooked chicken into ½-inch-thick (13 mm) slices.

PLAN AHEAD

1 Enjoy Chicken Teriyaki and Cucumber and Radish Sunomono for dinner, and have leftovers in tomorrow's bento.
2 Before you go to bed, set the timer on the rice cooker.
3 Reheat the Chicken Teriyaki in the morning.

BEEF ROLL-UP BENTO

A beef roll-up is a piece of thinly sliced beef that is rolled up with a vegetable inside and fried. We use raw okra here, but you can use all kinds of blanched vegetables. Ask a butcher to slice the beef paper thin, if you don't have a Japanese market nearby that sells packaged sukiyaki-cut beef. Or freeze a piece of round steak, defrost it lightly (half frozen), and slice it as thinly as possible.

TO MAKE THIS BENTO

Each bento has a main-dish recipe (below), side-dish recipes (page 163), and additional ingredients.

Beef Roll-Up with Okra (see recipe below)   Tamagoyaki (page 22)
Steamed Rice (page 18), with furikake of choice   Carrot Salad (page 181)

PREP TIME: 15 MINUTES   **COOK TIME:** 10 MINUTES   **YIELD:** 2 SERVINGS

BEEF ROLL-UP WITH OKRA

1 tablespoon (15 ml) soy sauce
1 tablespoon (15 ml) water
1½ teaspoons sugar
1½ teaspoons sake
5 ounces (150 g) beef (top round
    or sirloin), thinly sliced into
    6 slices
6 okra, stem end trimmed
1 teaspoon vegetable oil

1 In a small bowl, whisk together the soy sauce, water, sugar, and sake until the sugar dissolves completely. Set aside.

2 Lay a beef slice on a cutting board, add 1 piece of okra to the edge of the slice, and roll up. Repeat for the remaining 5 slices of beef.

3 Heat the oil in a large skillet over medium heat, place the roll-ups, seam sides down, in the pan, and cook while turning, until browned on all sides, 7 to 8 minutes. Reduce the heat to low and add the soy sauce mixture. Coat the meat well with the sauce.

4 Cut the rolls into halves or thirds crosswise.

PLAN AHEAD

1 Enjoy Beef Roll-Up and Carrot Salad for dinner, and have leftovers in tomorrow's bento. Alternatively, roll up the beef the night before and fry in the morning.
2 Before you go to bed, set the timer on the rice cooker.
3 In the morning, reheat or fry the prepped Beef-Roll Up and make the Tamagoyaki.

TSUKUNE BENTO

Tsukune are chicken meatballs, usually made with a teriyaki-style sweet and salty sauce. It is often served as 3 or 4 pieces skewered onto a bamboo stick at yakitori (skewered chicken) restaurants in Japan. It can be eaten as an appetizer, but it also works as a main dish for lunch or dinner.

TO MAKE THIS BENTO

Each bento has a main dish recipe (below), side-dish recipes (page 163), and additional ingredients.

Tsukune (see recipe below)
**Steamed Rice (page 18), with umeboshi
  (pickled sour plum)**

Sautéed Green Beans with Sesame Seeds (page 167)
Pickled Bell Pepper (page 201)
1 lettuce leaf

PREP TIME: 10 MINUTES   **COOK TIME:** 10 MINUTES   **YIELD:** 2 SERVINGS

TSUKUNE

SAUCE
1½ teaspoons sugar
1 tablespoon (15 ml) soy sauce
1 tablespoon (15 ml) mirin
2 tablespoons (30 ml) water
¼ teaspoon potato starch or
  cornstarch

MEATBALLS
½ pound (227 g) ground chicken
¼ yellow onion, finely chopped
1 egg yolk
½ teaspoon grated fresh ginger
¼ teaspoon salt
2 tablespoons (30 ml) potato
  starch or cornstarch
1 teaspoon vegetable oil, plus
  more for your hands

1 **To make the sauce:** In a small bowl, whisk together all the sauce ingredients. Set aside.

2 **To make the meatballs:** In a large bowl, combine the chicken, onion, egg yolk, ginger, salt, and potato starch until it is very sticky. Shape the meat mixture into 8 small balls or oval patties.

3 Heat the oil in a large skillet over medium heat. Cook the meatballs until browned, about 2 minutes. Turn the meat over, cover, and cook for about 3 minutes more, or until cooked through. Add the sauce and cook for a couple minutes, coating the meatballs with the thickened sauce.

PLAN AHEAD

1 Enjoy the Tsukune, Pickled Bell Pepper, and Sautéed Green Beans for dinner, and have leftovers for tomorrow's bento. Prep the meatballs by shaping them the night before (or freeze for later use), but don't fry.
2 Before you go to bed, wash and chop the lettuce and set the timer on the rice cooker.
3 In the morning, cook the meatballs and reheat the Sautéed Green Beans.

GRILLED MACKEREL BENTO

Grilled mackerel is a regular item packed in Japanese bento. When this salty but healthy dish is paired with rice, along with spinach ohitashi and tamagoyaki, you will have a nutritionally balanced lunch.

TO MAKE THIS BENTO

Each bento has a main-dish recipe (below), side-dish recipes (page 163), and additional ingredients.

Grilled Mackerel (see recipe below)
Steamed Rice (page 18), with furikake of choice
Spinach Ohitashi (page 175)

Tamagoyaki (page 22)
2 shiso leaves
4 grape tomatoes

PREP TIME: 15 MINUTES (OR UP TO OVERNIGHT IN THE REFRIGERATOR) **COOK TIME:** 8 MINUTES
YIELD: 2 SERVINGS

GRILLED MACKEREL

---

1 fillet (150 to 200 g) mackerel
  (half a mackerel)
Salt

1 Cut the fillet into quarters and liberally salt both sides of the fillets. Let sit for at least 15 minutes or up to overnight in the refrigerator. Pat dry with paper towels before cooking.

2 For a less smelly and easy-to-clean pan, line a large skillet with aluminum foil. Heat the pan over high heat. Reduce the heat to medium, and place the fish, skin side down, on the foil. Cook for about 4 minutes per side, or until browned and cooked through.

PLAN AHEAD

1 To prep the night before, salt and refrigerate the fish and make the Spinach Ohitashi.
2 Before you go to bed, set the timer on the rice cooker.
3 In the morning, make the Grilled Mackerel and Tamagoyaki.

BEEF SHIGURENI BENTO

Beef shigureni is thinly sliced beef cooked in a sweet and salty sauce with ginger. This strongly flavored beef lasts for up to a week in the refrigerator, establishing it as a great make-ahead dish for bento. Any cut of beef will work, such as tri-tip, or you may prefer meat with a little fat. Thinly slicing raw beef by hand can be difficult, so partially freeze it first; the firmer beef will be much easier to slice.

TO MAKE THIS BENTO

Each bento has a main-dish recipe (below), side-dish recipes (page 163), and additional ingredients.

Beef Shigureni (see recipe below)
Steamed Rice (page 18), with furikake of choice and umeboshi (pickled sour plum)
Sautéed Shimeji Mushrooms with Soy Butter Sauce (page 189)

Snap Peas and Egg Salad (page 183)
4 to 6 blanched carrot flowers
2 lettuce leaves

PREP TIME: 5 MINUTES   COOK TIME: 40 MINUTES   YIELD: 2 SERVINGS

BEEF SHIGURENI

½ pound (227 g) beef (such as tri-tip), thinly sliced
1-inch (2.5 cm) piece fresh ginger, sliced into matchsticks (1½ inches, or 4 cm, long)
½ cup (120 ml) water
2 tablespoons (30 ml) soy sauce
1 tablespoon (15 ml) sugar
1½ teaspoons sake
1½ teaspoons mirin

1 Cut the thinly sliced beef into bite-size pieces.

2 Combine the water, soy sauce, sugar, sake, mirin, and ginger in a medium saucepan, and cook over medium heat until boiling. Add the beef and stir, breaking apart the meat with a spoon so it doesn't stick together. Bring the mixture to a boil and skim the fat.

3 Cover and cook for 25 to 30 minutes over medium-low heat. Uncover and continue cooking until the liquid has mostly evaporated.

PLAN AHEAD

1 Make the Beef Shigureni anytime, up to a week ahead.
2 The night before, hard-boil an egg, blanch the snap peas and carrot flowers, and wash and chop the lettuce.
3 Before you go to bed, set the timer on the rice cooker.
4 In the morning, make the Sautéed Shimeji Mushrooms and reheat the Beef Shigureni.

SUKIYAKI BENTO

Sukiyaki is a popular hot pot dish with beef and vegetables. It is seasoned with soy sauce and sugar, and the sweet and salty flavor goes well with rice. It is traditionally cooked in an iron pot on a portable burner and eaten at the dinner table as it cooks. Here, the dish is cooked in a skillet. When eaten in Japan, sukiyaki is dipped in raw egg, but this recipe calls for a soft-boiled egg. To easily slice the beef, partially freeze it first.

TO MAKE THIS BENTO

Each bento has a main-dish recipe (below), side-dish recipes (page 163), and additional ingredients.

Sukiyaki (see recipe below)
Steamed Rice (page 18), with sesame seeds

Shungiku Salad (page 182)
1 soft-boiled egg

PREP TIME: 7 MINUTES   **COOK TIME:** 10 MINUTES   **YIELD:** 2 SERVINGS

SUKIYAKI

½ bunch (3.5 ounces, or 100 g) enoki mushrooms

4 shiitake mushrooms

5 ounces (150 g) beef (preferably rib-eye or chuck eye roll), thinly sliced

½ teaspoon vegetable oil

1 naganegi (long white onion) or 4 green onions, sliced on the diagonal

¼ medium or firm tofu block (3.5 ounces, or 100 g), cut into 6 to 8 pieces

1½ tablespoons (23 ml) soy sauce

1 tablespoon (15 ml) sugar

1 tablespoon (15 ml) sake

1 Trim the bottoms of the enoki mushrooms and separate into small bunches. Remove and discard the shiitake mushroom stems and make shallow cuts on the caps to decorate with star shapes. Cut the sliced beef into 3-inch-wide (7.5 cm) pieces.

2 Heat the oil in a large skillet over medium heat. Add the beef and cook until browned slightly. Add all the remaining ingredients to the pan and stir to combine. Reduce the heat to medium-low, cover, and cook for 4 to 5 minutes, or until cooked through.

3 Remove the lid, turn the vegetables, cook for another couple minutes, and then remove from the heat.

PLAN AHEAD

1 Enjoy Sukiyaki for dinner, and have leftovers in tomorrow's bento. Alternatively, cut up all the ingredients the night before to cook in the morning.

2 Shungiku Salad also can be made the night before, but the color may change a little.

3 Before you go to bed, set the timer on the rice cooker.

4 In the morning, reheat or make the Sukiyaki and soft-boil the egg.

SALMON TERIYAKI BENTO

This classic salmon teriyaki is simple to make in a skillet. The fish does not need to be marinated, yet it still comes out flavorful. Pack the fish next to or on top of the rice in the bento box so that the rice will soak up the great flavor of the sauce.

TO MAKE THIS BENTO

Each bento has a main-dish recipe (below), side-dish recipes (page 163), and additional ingredients.

Salmon Teriyaki (see recipe below)
Steamed Rice (page 18)
Daikon and Carrot Nimono (page 169)

Blanched broccoli
Hard-boiled egg

PREP TIME: 5 MINUTES   **COOK TIME:** 15 MINUTES   **YIELD:** 2 SERVINGS

SALMON TERIYAKI

2 tablespoons (30 ml) soy sauce
1 tablespoon (15 ml) sugar
1 tablespoon (15 ml) sake
1 tablespoon (15 ml) mirin
1 teaspoon vegetable oil
2 salmon fillets (3.5 ounces, or 100 g, each)

1 In a small bowl, combine the soy sauce, sugar, sake, and mirin. Set aside.

2 Heat the oil in a medium skillet over medium-high heat. Add the salmon and cook until browned, 4 to 5 minutes per side.

3 Reduce the heat to medium and add the teriyaki sauce to the pan. Spoon some sauce over the salmon to coat it and cook until the sauce is reduced.

PLAN AHEAD

1 Daikon and Carrot Nimono can be made ahead of time and kept in the refrigerator for up to 3 days.
2 Enjoy Salmon Teriyaki for dinner, and have leftovers in tomorrow's bento.
3 Hard-boil the egg and blanch the broccoli the night before.
4 Before you go to bed, set the timer on the rice cooker.
5 In the morning, reheat or make the Salmon Teriyaki.

PORK SHOGAYAKI BENTO

Shogayaki is similar to teriyaki but with a kick of freshly grated ginger (*shoga*). It is one of the most popular home-cooked meals for lunch, dinner, and bento in Japan. We tend to use very thinly sliced pork for shogayaki, but thin-cut boneless pork chops that are found at any supermarket are also fine to use. You can cut the pork into pieces after cooking to make it easier to fit in a bento box and eat with chopsticks.

TO MAKE THIS BENTO

Each bento has a main-dish recipe (below), side-dish recipes (page 163), and additional ingredients.

Pork Shogayaki (see recipe below)
Steamed Rice (page 18), with furikake of choice
 and umeboshi (pickled sour plum)

Bean Sprouts and Bell Pepper Namul (page 182)
Satsumaimo Amani (page 174)
1 or 2 lettuce leaves

PREP TIME: 3 MINUTES **COOK TIME:** 7 MINUTES **YIELD:** 2 SERVINGS

PORK SHOGAYAKI

1½ tablespoons (23 ml) mirin
1 tablespoon (15 ml) soy sauce
1 tablespoon (15 ml) sake
1 teaspoon grated ginger
1 teaspoon vegetable oil
4 thin-cut boneless pork chops,
 about ¼ inch (6 mm) thick

1 In a small bowl, whisk together the mirin, soy sauce, sake, and ginger. Set aside.

2 Heat the oil in a large skillet over medium-high heat. Add the pork chops and cook until browned, about 3 minutes per side.

3 Add the ginger sauce to the pan and cook for a minute to coat the meat with the sauce.

PLAN AHEAD

1 The Bean Sprouts and Bell Pepper Namul and Satsumaimo Amani can be made the day before and kept in the refrigerator.
2 The Pork Shogayaki can be prepared the night before or in the morning.
3 Before you go to bed, set the timer on the rice cooker.
4 In the morning, reheat or make the Pork Shogayaki.

SANDWICH BENTO

TONKATSU SANDWICH BENTO

Tonkatsu is a bread crumb–coated, deep-fried pork cutlet that is a popular dinner entrée in Japan. And the tonkatsu sandwich is one of the most popular sandwiches in Japan. With the additions of Japanese mayo, tonkatsu sauce, and lots of cabbage, this sandwich is a complete, delicious meal in your hand.

TO MAKE THIS BENTO

Each bento has a main-dish recipe (below), side-dish recipes (page 163), and additional ingredients.

Tonkatsu Sandwich (see recipe below)	**Celery and yellow pepper sticks**
Seasonal fruits	**Dressing of choice**

PREP TIME: 10 MINUTES   **COOK TIME:** 10 MINUTES   **YIELD:** 2 SERVINGS

TONKATSU SANDWICH

2 pork chops, ½ inch (13 mm) thick

Salt and black pepper, to taste

¼ cup (30 g) all-purpose flour

1 large egg, beaten

1 cup (50 g) panko

Vegetable oil, for frying

4 slices sandwich bread (preferably thinly sliced shokupan)

2 tablespoons (28 g) Japanese mayonnaise

1 cup (70 g) thinly shredded cabbage

2 tablespoons (30 g) tonkatsu sauce (or equal parts ketchup and Worcestershire sauce)

1 Pound the pork chops with a meat mallet a few times, then make small cuts all over the surface with the tip of a sharp knife. Season both sides of the meat with salt and pepper. Coat the meat lightly with the flour, dip in the beaten egg, and dredge in the panko.

2 Heat 1 inch (2.5 cm) of oil to 350°F (180°C) over medium-high heat in a large skillet. Add the pork chops and fry until golden brown and the meat floats to the surface, 6 to 8 minutes, turning once or twice. Transfer the meat to a cooling rack for a minute.

3 Spread 1 tablespoon (14 g) of the mayo on a slice of bread. Top with ½ cup (35 g) of the cabbage. Place the pork chop on the cabbage and drizzle with 1 tablespoon (15 g) of the tonkatsu sauce. Top with the other slice of bread. Repeat to make a second sandwich. Cut off the crusts if you prefer. Wrap the sandwiches tightly in plastic wrap, then cut them in half.

PLAN AHEAD

1 Prepare the Tonkatsu through step 1 and prep the vegetable sticks the night before.
2 In the morning, fry the Tonkatsu and assemble the sandwiches.

ANTIPASTO BENTO

An antipasto plate filled with cured meats, cheese, and vegetables dressed in oil and vinegar is a typical starter of an Italian meal, but it also can be a balanced, tasty, and fun bento lunch. You should pack the bruschetta (grilled bread) and salad separately in divided sections to keep the bread crispy.

TO MAKE THIS BENTO

Each bento has a main-dish recipe (below), side-dish recipes (page 163), and additional ingredients.

Bruschetta with Caprese Salad (see recipe below)
Marinated Asparagus (page 176)
Lunch meat (prosciutto, salami, and mortadella)

Seasonal fruits
Dried fruits (such as apricots)
Almonds

PREP TIME: 5 MINUTES   **COOK TIME:** 5 MINUTES   **YIELD:** 2 SERVINGS

ANTIPASTO WITH CAPRESE SALAD

BRUSCHETTA

⅓ to ½ baguette, sliced ½ inch (13 mm) thick
1 tablespoon (15 ml) extra-virgin olive oil
Salt, to taste

CAPRESE SALAD

1 cup (150 g) grape tomatoes, halved
10 fresh mini mozzarella balls, halved
6 leaves fresh basil, thinly sliced
2 teaspoons extra-virgin olive oil
1 teaspoon balsamic vinegar
¼ teaspoon salt
Black pepper, to taste

1 Preheat the oven to 425°F (220°C).

2 **To make the bruschetta:** Brush both sides of the baguette slices with the olive oil and sprinkle with salt. Place on a baking sheet, transfer to the oven, and bake for 5 minutes.

3 **To make the caprese salad:** Combine all the salad ingredients in a medium bowl.

PLAN AHEAD

1 Make the Caprese Salad and Marinated Asparagus the night before.
2 In the morning, pop the sliced baguette in the oven while you are eating breakfast. (A day-old baguette will still make tasty and crispy bruschetta.)

MIXED SANDWICHES BENTO

Mixed sandwiches ("mix sando" in Japanese) are a combination of sandwiches made with white bread, egg salad, ham, cheese, and vegetables, such as cucumber, lettuce, and tomatoes. Almost all traditional Japanese coffee houses, called *kissaten*, serve these crustless sandwiches for lunch or as a light meal. They are also sold at convenience stores in Japan.

TO MAKE THIS BENTO

Each bento has a main-dish recipe (below), side-dish recipes (page 163), and additional ingredients.

Mixed Sandwiches (see recipe below)　　　　**Grape tomatoes**
Buttered Broccoli (page 168)

PREP TIME: 10 MINUTES　　　**COOK TIME:** 5 MINUTES　　　**YIELD:** 2 SERVINGS

MIXED SANDWICHES

1 Persian or ¼ English
　cucumber, thinly sliced
Pinch salt, plus more for
　sprinkling
Butter, at room temperature
6 slices sandwich bread
1 hard-boiled egg, peeled
　and chopped
1 tablespoon (14 g) plus
　½ teaspoon mayonnaise
1 slice cheese of choice
2 slices ham
1 lettuce leaf

1　Sprinkle the cucumber with salt and let sit for 5 minutes. Pat dry with a paper towel.

2　Spread the butter on one side of each slice of bread.

3　Mix the hard-boiled egg with 1 tablespoon (14 g) of the mayonnaise and the remaining pinch of salt.

4　On one slice of bread, butter side up, place the cheese and cucumber slices, and top with another slice of bread, butter side down. For the second sandwich, spread the remaining ½ teaspoon mayonnaise on the butter side of a slice of bread, top with the ham, lettuce, and another slice of bread, butter side down. Make a third sandwich with the egg salad.

5　Cut off the crusts and slice the sandwiches in half.

PLAN AHEAD

1　Make the hard-boiled egg the night before and refrigerate it until the morning.
2　In the morning, prepare the Mixed Sandwiches and Buttered Broccoli.

CUCUMBER AND CREAM CHEESE SANDWICH BENTO

These classic sandwiches served at afternoon tea are easy to make with only three ingredients and can be quite tasty in bento. Be sure to salt the cucumber slices to release the water before making the sandwiches or they will end up being soggy. The salt also helps add flavor to the sandwiches. If made right, these creamy and crunchy sandwiches will become a new favorite.

TO MAKE THIS BENTO

Each bento has a main-dish recipe (below), side-dish recipes (page 163), and additional ingredients.

Cucumber and Cream Cheese Sandwiches
    (see recipe below)
Sautéed Green Peas and Sausage (page 198)

Seasonal fruits
1 large lettuce leaf

PREP TIME: 12 MINUTES   **YIELD:** 2 SERVINGS

CUCUMBER AND CREAM CHEESE SANDWICHES

½ English cucumber, thinly
    sliced (2 mm thick)
4 ounces (113 g) cream cheese
¼ teaspoon salt
4 slices sandwich bread

1 Place the cucumber slices in a shallow dish and sprinkle evenly with salt on both sides. Set aside for 5 minutes to allow the cucumber to release water. Place the cucumber slices on layers of paper towel and press gently with another paper towel to remove excess moisture.

2 Spread the cream cheese on one side of each slice of bread. Top with 2 layers of cucumber slices, and then place another slice of bread, cream cheese–side down, on top to make a sandwich.

3 Cut off the crusts and slice the sandwiches to fit in the bento box.

PLAN AHEAD

1 You can make the Sautéed Green Peas and Sausage a day in advance.
2 In the morning, prepare the sandwiches and reheat the Sautéed Green Peas and Sausage.

HAMBURGER BENTO

The hamburger is a classic American dish that can be easily made at home. You can change the toppings to anything you desire. The side dish of Asian Coleslaw has a lighter and fresher taste with a rice vinegar dressing instead of a mayo-based dressing. Add the fruit and snap peas for a perfect lunch.

TO MAKE THIS BENTO

Each bento has a main-dish recipe (below), side-dish recipes (page 163), and additional ingredients.

Hamburger (see recipe below)
Asian Coleslaw (page 183)
12 to 14 blanched snap peas

4 to 6 cornichons
Pineapple and blueberry cup

PREP TIME: 10 MINUTES   **COOK TIME:** 10 MINUTES   **YIELD:** 2 SERVINGS

HAMBURGER

½ pound (227 g) ground beef
¼ teaspoon salt
Pinch black pepper
1 teaspoon vegetable oil
2 hamburger buns
1 tablespoon (15 g) ketchup
1 tablespoon (15 g) mustard
4 thin slices red onion
2 thick slices tomato
2 lettuce leaves
1 tablespoon (14 g) mayonnaise

1 Combine the ground beef, salt, and pepper in a medium bowl. Divide the mixture in half and form into 2 balls. Flatten the balls to make patties slightly bigger than the size of the buns, making a dent in the middle of each patty.

2 Heat the oil in a medium skillet over medium heat. Add the 2 patties and cook, 4 to 5 minutes per side.

3 On the bottom halves of the buns, spread ½ tablespoon each of the ketchup and mustard. Top each bottom bun with a cooked hamburger, 2 onion slices, 1 tomato slice, and 1 lettuce leaf. Then spread ½ tablespoon each of the mayo on the top halves of the buns and place them on the lettuce.

PLAN AHEAD

1 You can make the Asian Coleslaw a day before if you don't mind it being a little softer.
2 Enjoy Hamburgers for dinner and leave uncooked patties for tomorrow's bento. Blanch the snap peas the night before.
3 In the morning, cook the Hamburgers.

SUSHI AND ONIGIRI BENTO

SUSHI BURRITO BENTO

A sushi burrito is a big sushi roll eaten like a burrito. Technicalities aside, it is a convenient way to eat sushi (no chopsticks!) and you can put anything you like in the roll. For the bento, avoid adding any raw meat or fish. Here, we used leftover pieces of karaage (fried chicken) with some thinly sliced veggies, pickled ginger, and sriracha mayo. Be creative and find your favorite flavor combination!

TO MAKE THIS BENTO

Each bento has a main-dish recipe (below), side-dish recipes (page 163), and additional ingredients.

Sushi Burrito (see recipe below)　　　　　**Seasonal fruit**
Edamame (page 172)

PREP TIME: 5 MINUTES　　　**COOK TIME:** 13 MINUTES　　　**YIELD:** 2 SERVINGS

SUSHI BURRITO

2 sheets nori

2 cups (330 g) Sushi Rice (page 164)

6 to 8 pieces Chicken Karaage (page 74)

1 small cucumber, cut into matchsticks

1 green onion, diagonally sliced

½ medium carrot, cut into matchsticks

2 tablespoons (20 g) benishoga (pickled red ginger)

1 tablespoon (14 g) mayonnaise

1 tablespoon (15 g) sriracha sauce

1 Place a bamboo sushi mat on your work surface with the bamboo slats running left to right. Place a sheet of nori on the sushi mat and spread half of the sushi rice on the nori, leaving a 1-inch (2.5 cm) border along the far edge of the nori.

2 In the center of the sushi rice, place half each of the karaage, cucumber, green onion, and carrot. Holding the filling down, roll from the side closest to you toward the other side, guiding with the sushi mat, as if you were rolling a jelly-roll cake. Gently squeeze to tighten. Wrap the roll in parchment paper and diagonally cut in half. Repeat with the second sheet of nori and the remaining ingredients.

3 Mix the mayonnaise and sriracha sauce and pour into a sauce container with a lid. (If you are eating right away, you can pour the sauce on the fillings before rolling the sushi burrito.)

PLAN AHEAD

1 Enjoy Karaage for dinner and save some to fill the burrito for tomorrow's bento. You can also make the Edamame and cut up the veggies for the burrito the night before.
2 Before you go to bed, set the timer on the rice cooker.
3 In the morning, make the Sushi Burrito.

ONIGIRI BENTO

Onigiri is soul food for Japanese people and a staple carbohydrate dish for bento. These shaped rice balls are filled with various ingredients and wrapped with nori. The fillings are often strongly flavored seafood or vegetables that go with unseasoned rice. Alternatively, instead of putting a filling inside, seasonings or fillings are mixed into the rice and then the rice is shaped into balls. Or, if you choose no filling or nori, simply flavor with some salt.

TO MAKE THIS BENTO

Each bento has a main-dish recipe (below), side-dish recipes (page 163), and additional ingredients.

Onigiri (see recipe below) with choice of filling:
- **Salmon Flakes (see recipe below)**
- **Kombu Tsukudani (page 188)**
- **Okaka (page 184)**
- **Umeboshi (pickled sour plum), pitted**

Miso Eggplant and Shishito Peppers (page 170)
Tamagoyaki with Green Onions (page 22)
40 blueberries
2 lettuce leaves

PREP TIME: 10 MINUTES   **COOK TIME:** 20 MINUTES   **YIELD:** 2 SERVINGS

ONIGIRI WITH SALMON FLAKES

SALMON FLAKES
¼ pound (113 g) salmon fillet
1½ teaspoons sake
1 teaspoon mirin
½ teaspoon salt

ONIGIRI
2 cups (330 g) Steamed Rice (page 18)
Salt
4 sheets nori, about 2 × 4 inches (5 × 10 cm)

1 **To make the salmon flakes:** Bake the salmon in a toaster or conventional oven at 400ºF to 450ºF (200ºC to 230ºC) for 7 to 8 minutes (do not brown the fish).

2 Break the fish into smaller pieces and remove any bones and skin.

3 Heat a nonstick medium skillet over medium-low heat. Add the salmon and sake, and cook, breaking up bigger pieces and stirring constantly, until the fish looks drier, 5 to 6 minutes. Add the mirin and salt to the skillet, and cook for a few more minutes.

4 **To make the onigiri:** Set the rice aside for a few minutes until it is cool enough to handle. Wet your hands with water and sprinkle with salt. Place one-quarter of the cooled rice in one hand, then use both hands to press and form the rice into a triangle shape.

5 Make a well in the middle of the rice ball and put a teaspoon or two of the filling in the well. Close the well. Reshape into a triangle as needed and wrap with a sheet of nori, wrapping it around one side of the triangle. Repeat to make the 3 remaining onigiri.

6 Store the salmon flakes in a clean airtight container for up to a week or freeze for up to 3 weeks.

PLAN AHEAD

1 If you would like Salmon Flakes or Kombu Tsukudani for the Onigiri, make them in advance.
2 The night before, make the Miso Eggplant and Shishito Peppers.
3 Before you go to bed, set the timer for the rice cooker.
4 In the morning, make the Onigiri and Tamagoyaki with Aonori, and reheat the Miso Eggplant and Shishito Peppers.

SUSHI ROLL BENTO

These sushi rolls are simply filled with either cucumber or sausage. You can change the fillings to whatever you like; however, choose cooked ingredients rather than raw fish because the bento may be sitting for a few hours at room temperature before lunch.

TO MAKE THIS BENTO

Each bento has a main-dish recipe (below), side-dish recipes (page 163), and additional ingredients.

Sushi Roll (see recipe below)
Tuna and Potato Nimono (page 186)

Stir-Fried Bean Sprouts and Red Pepper (page 177)
Cut-up Asian pear

PREP TIME: 5 MINUTES   **COOK TIME:** 10 MINUTES   **YIELD:** 2 SERVINGS

SUSHI ROLL

2 sheets nori, 8 × 7½ inches
　(21 × 19 cm)
3 to 4 smoked sausages, boiled
1 Japanese cucumber or
　2 Persian cucumbers
1⅓ cups (266 g) Sushi Rice
　(page 164)
Soy sauce, for serving

1　Cut the sheets of nori in half lengthwise. Cut the boiled sausages and cucumber to make pieces ½ inch (13 mm) thick and 7½ inches (19 cm) long (using multiple pieces to get the length is okay).

2　Place a bamboo sushi mat on your work surface with the bamboo slats running left to right. Place a sheet of nori on the sushi mat with the long side close to the edge of the mat (the edge near you). Spread about ⅓ cup (65 g) of the sushi rice on the nori sheet, leaving a 1-inch (2.5 cm) border along the far edge of the nori.

3　Place half of the sausages lined up across the middle of the rice, running left to right. Holding the filling down, roll from the side closest to you toward the other side, as if you were rolling a jelly-roll cake. Pull the mat to tighten the roll. Make a second roll with the remaining sausage. Then make 2 cucumber rolls the same way. Cut each roll into 6 pieces. Serve with soy sauce.

PLAN AHEAD

1　Prep the fillings and make the Tuna and Potato Nimono and Stir-Fried Bean Sprouts and Red Pepper the night before.
2　Before you go to bed, set the timer for the rice cooker.
3　In the morning, make the Sushi Rolls, reheat the Stir-Fried Bean Sprouts and Red Pepper, and cut up the pear.

SPAM MUSUBI BENTO

Spam musubi, a rice ball with grilled Spam, is a popular Hawaiian dish that is also popular in Japan, especially in the regions near US military bases. This salty canned meat goes surprisingly well with steamed rice. Even if this may not be something you eat every day, it might satisfy a guilty salt craving every so often. You should try it at least once if you haven't already.

TO MAKE THIS BENTO

Each bento has a main-dish recipe (below), side-dish recipes (page 163), and additional ingredients.

Spam Musubi (rice ball with processed meat; see recipe below)
Daikon and Lemon Namasu (page 200)

Tamagoyaki with Benishoga (page 22)
6 blanched broccoli florets
Grapes

PREP TIME: 5 MINUTES   COOK TIME: 8 MINUTES   YIELD: 2 SERVINGS

SPAM MUSUBI

4 slices Spam, cut into ½-inch-thick (13 mm) pieces
2 cups (330 g) Steamed Rice (page 18)
4 pieces nori, cut into ½ × 8-inch (13 mm × 20 cm) strips

1 Cook the Spam in a large skillet over medium heat for 2 to 3 minutes per side.

2 Meanwhile, wet your hands, take one-quarter of the steamed rice (make sure it is cool enough to handle), and make a rice ball about the size and shape of the meat. Repeat to make the 3 remaining rice balls.

3 Place 1 piece of meat on a rice ball and wrap with a nori strip. Repeat with the 3 remaining rice balls.

PLAN AHEAD

1 The night before, make the Daikon and Lemon Namasu and blanch the broccoli.
2 Before you go to bed, set the timer for the rice cooker.
3 In the morning, make the Spam Musubi and Tamagoyaki with Benishoga.

INARI SUSHI BENTO

Inari sushi is a sushi rice ball stuffed in seasoned *aburaage*, a deep-fried tofu sushi pouch. It is portable and perfect for bento as the ingredients are fully cooked and well seasoned (no need to dip in soy sauce!). Simple inari sushi with only aburaage and sushi rice is great, but here we dressed them with cut-out flower-shaped carrot slices and snow pea leaves on a bed of thinly cooked and shredded egg (Kinshi Tamago, page 194) for decoration.

TO MAKE THIS BENTO

Each bento has a main-dish recipe (below), side-dish recipes (page 163), and additional ingredients.

Inari Sushi (see recipe below)   **Strawberries**
Ham-Wrapped Asparagus (page 197)

PREP TIME: 20 MINUTES   **COOK TIME:** 20 MINUTES   **YIELD:** 2 SERVINGS

INARI SUSHI

8 squares aburaage (or
    4 rectangles cut in half)
2 cups (475 ml) water
¼ cup (50 g) sugar
3 tablespoons (45 ml)
    soy sauce
Salt
2 cups (330 g) Sushi Rice
    (page 164)
Kinshi Tamago (page 194),
    thinly sliced
Blanched carrot flowers and
    snow peas cut into leaf
    shapes, for garnish

1 Bring a medium saucepan of water to a boil.

2 Roll the aburaage with a rolling pin a couple times to flatten it. Cut one side of each aburaage, then carefully open to make a pouch.

3 Reduce the heat to medium-low and cook the prepared aburaage for 1 minute. Drain well.

4 In a large pot, add the 2 cups (475 ml) water, sugar, and soy sauce, and bring to a boil. Add the aburaage and cook for 10 minutes. Remove from the heat and let the aburaage cool completely in the broth.

5 Wet your hands and sprinkle with salt. Place about ¼ cup (40 g) of cooled sushi rice in one hand, then use two hands to form an oblong rice ball. (Adjust the size to fit in the aburaage pouch.) Repeat to make the 7 remaining rice balls.

6 Squeeze the aburaage just a little to remove some of the liquid and stuff the rice balls in the pouches. On the open side of the pouch, place the kinshi tamago threads, flower-shaped carrots, and snow peas.

PLAN AHEAD

1 Seasoned aburaage tastes even better the next day, so cook it the day before and refrigerate in the broth overnight. The Kinshi Tamago and vegetable garnish also can be prepared ahead of time. Prep the Ham-Wrapped Asparagus but leave the frying until the morning.

2 Before you go to bed, set the timer of the rice cooker.

3 In the morning, make the sushi rice balls and stuff them in the aburaage and cook the Ham-Wrapped Asparagus.

YAKI ONIGIRI BENTO

Yaki onigiri is a grilled onigiri rice ball brushed with soy sauce. Crispy grilled rice with lightly sweetened and browned soy sauce creates an irresistible aroma while grilling. Though browning the onigiri on a grill is best (which is why they are a popular barbecue food), yaki onigiri also can be made easily in a skillet. It also freezes well (up to 1 month), making yaki onigiri a great afternoon snack for kids or a quick carbohydrate to add to your bento box.

TO MAKE THIS BENTO

Each bento has a main-dish recipe (below), side-dish recipes (page 163), and additional ingredients.

Yaki Onigiri (see recipe below)   **Tamagoyaki (page 22)**
Marinated Shrimp and Vegetables (page 187)

PREP TIME: 5 MINUTES   **COOK TIME:** 13 MINUTES   **YIELD:** 2 SERVINGS

YAKI ONIGIRI

1 tablespoon (15 ml) soy sauce
1 teaspoon mirin
½ teaspoon vegetable oil
Onigiri (page 165)

1 In a small bowl, mix together the soy sauce and mirin. Set aside.

2 Heat the oil in a large skillet over medium heat, wiping off excess oil with paper towels. Place the onigiri in the pan and cook for 4 to 5 minutes per side, or until lightly browned.

3 Brush the soy sauce–mirin mixture on the onigiri and cook for 1 minute more on each side.

PLAN AHEAD

1 While freshly made Yaki Onigiri taste the best, they can be wrapped individually in plastic wrap and kept in the freezer for up to 1 month.

2 Make the Marinated Shrimp and Vegetables the day before.

3 In the morning, reheat the frozen Yaki Onigiri in a microwave or toaster oven and make the Tamagoyaki with Ham.

NOODLE BENTO

RAMEN BENTO

Making homemade ramen noodle soup from scratch can be time-consuming, but this simple soup made with store-bought chicken broth is surprisingly tasty with a few key ingredients such as fresh ginger, garlic, and sesame oil. Use the low-sodium broth and then add enough miso and soy sauce for more flavor.

TO MAKE THIS BENTO

Each bento has a main-dish recipe (below), side-dish recipes (page 163), and additional ingredients.

Miso Ramen (see recipe below)

PREP TIME: 10 MINUTES   **COOK TIME:** 10 MINUTES   **YIELD:** 2 SERVINGS

MISO RAMEN

3 cups (710 ml) low-sodium chicken broth

1- to 1½-inch (2.5 to 4 cm) piece fresh ginger, peeled and thinly sliced

1 clove garlic, smashed

2 green onions (1 cut in half for the soup and 1 chopped for garnish), divided

2 tablespoons (32 g) miso

1 tablespoon (15 ml) soy sauce

1 tablespoon (15 ml) mirin

1 teaspoon sesame oil

2 bundles/packets (3 ounces, or 85 g) dried ramen noodles

2 hard-boiled eggs, halved

1 cup (50 g) bean sprouts, blanched

6 snow peas, blanched

2 to 4 slices ham

1 In a medium saucepan, add the chicken broth, ginger, garlic, and halved green onion, and bring to a boil. Simmer for 3 minutes and then discard the ginger, garlic, and green onion.

2 Add the miso, soy sauce, and mirin, and return to a boil. Add the sesame oil and remove from the heat. Immediately transfer the soup to insulated jars.

3 Boil the ramen noodles according to package directions, drain, and transfer to a bento box large enough to hold the noodles, toppings, and soup. Top with the hard-boiled eggs, bean sprouts, snow peas, ham, and chopped green onions.

4 When you are ready to eat, pour the soup over the noodles and toppings.

PLAN AHEAD

1 Prepare the Miso Ramen the day before through step 2 and refrigerate. Hard-boil the eggs and blanch the bean sprouts and snow peas the night before.

2 In the morning, boil the ramen noodles, reheat the broth, and prep any toppings.

SOBA NOODLE SALAD BENTO

Soba noodles are made from buckwheat flour and have nutrients, such as vitamin B, minerals, and fiber. They are not only healthy but also quite delicious because of the nutty buckwheat flavor. This salad is tossed in a soy sauce–based dressing with shredded white chicken meat and thinly sliced crunchy vegetables. You can use any vegetables you like.

TO MAKE THIS BENTO

Each bento has a main-dish recipe (below), side-dish recipes (page 163), and additional ingredients.

Soba Noodle Salad (see recipe below)　　　　**Seasonal fruits**
Sautéed Shiitake Mushrooms (page 192)

PREP TIME: 1 HOUR　　**COOK TIME:** 20 MINUTES　　**YIELD:** 2 TO 4 SERVINGS

SOBA NOODLE SALAD

5 to 7 ounces (150 to 200 g)
　　dried soba noodles
2 chicken tenderloins
1 tablespoon (15 ml) sake
¼ cup (60 ml) Mentsuyu
　　(page 204)
2 teaspoons rice vinegar
1 teaspoon sesame oil
1 Persian cucumber or
　　⅓ English cucumber,
　　julienned
½ medium carrot, julienned
¼ medium red bell pepper,
　　julienned
1 or 2 green onions, chopped

1　Bring a medium saucepan of water to a boil. Cook the soba according to the package directions. Rinse under running water and drain well.

2　While the soba is cooking, place the chicken tenderloins in a microwave-safe dish and sprinkle with the sake. Cover and microwave for 3 minutes, flipping halfway through. Shred the cooked chicken using 2 forks.

3　In a large bowl, mix together the mentsuyu, rice vinegar, and sesame oil.

4　Add the chicken, soba, and vegetables, and combine well.

PLAN AHEAD

1　Mentsuyu can be made in advance and kept in the refrigerator for up to 2 to 3 weeks. Prep the chicken, dressing, vegetables, and Sautéed Shiitake Mushrooms the night before.

2　In the morning, cook the noodles and assemble the salad.

BUKKAKE UDON BENTO

Bukkake udon is chilled udon noodles served with an umami-packed sauce and toppings of choice, such as green onions, grated ginger, egg, and tempura. The carrot kakiage in this dish is an easy tempura and great as a topping on chilled noodles. Pack the cooked noodles, toppings, and sauce separately. Put the toppings on the noodles and pour the sauce over everything before eating.

TO MAKE THIS BENTO

Each bento has a main-dish recipe (below), side-dish recipes (page 163), and additional ingredients.

Carrot Kakiage (see recipe below)
Mentsuyu (page 204), diluted with water
    (1 part Mentsuyu, 2 parts water)
1 hard-boiled egg

1 green onion, chopped
1 teaspoon grated fresh ginger
Udon noodles, boiled according to package
    directions and chilled

PREP TIME: 10 MINUTES   **COOK TIME:** 10 MINUTES   **YIELD:** 2 SERVINGS

CARROT KAKIAGE

¼ cup (30 g) plus 2 teaspoons
    cake flour or fine pastry
    flour, divided
Pinch salt
1 medium carrot, peeled and
    cut into matchsticks
¼ onion, thinly sliced
¼ cup (60 ml) cold water
Vegetable oil, for frying

1 In a medium bowl, combine the 2 teaspoons of flour and the salt, and coat the sliced carrot and onion.

2 In a small bowl, mix the remaining ¼ cup (30 g) flour and the cold water and add to the carrot mixture.

3 Heat 2 inches (5 cm) of oil in a small skillet over medium-high heat. Divide the carrot-onion mixture into 4 parts and drop in the hot oil using a spoon. Fry for 4 to 5 minutes, turning once or twice. Remove from the pan with a slotted spoon and place on a paper towel–lined plate to absorb excess oil.

PLAN AHEAD

1 Mentsuyu can be made in advance and kept in an airtight container in the refrigerator for up to 2 to 3 weeks.

2 Make the Carrot Kakiage, hard-boil an egg, cook the udon noodles, chop the green onion, and grate the ginger the night before. Refrigerate.

3 In the morning, reheat the Carrot Kakiage in a toaster or conventional oven and assemble the bukkake udon.

SHRIMP AVOCADO PASTA SALAD BENTO

Shrimp, avocado, and pasta are tossed with a lemon and soy sauce–based dressing with a kick of wasabi for this dish. The only challenge is waiting until lunchtime to eat this irresistible salad!

TO MAKE THIS BENTO

Each bento has a main-dish recipe (below), side-dish recipes (page 163), and additional ingredients.

Shrimp Avocado Pasta Salad
  (see recipe below)

Fresh Fruits Jelly (page 205)

PREP TIME: 15 MINUTES   **COOK TIME:** 10 MINUTES   **YIELD:** 2 SERVINGS

SHRIMP AVOCADO PASTA SALAD

¼ pound (115 g) dried short pasta
1 teaspoon plus ¼ teaspoon salt, divided
¼ pound (115 g) raw shrimp, peeled and deveined
1 tablespoon (14 g) mayonnaise
1 tablespoon (15 ml) freshly squeezed lemon juice
½ teaspoon soy sauce
½ teaspoon wasabi paste, plus more to taste
Black pepper, to taste
1 avocado, pitted, peeled, and cubed
10 grape tomatoes, halved
¼ cup (15 g) chopped parsley
1 cup (20 g) baby spinach

1 In a medium saucepan of boiling water, cook the pasta with 1 teaspoon of the salt. A few minutes before the end of the cook time, add the shrimp and cook through. Drain and rinse under cold water.

2 In a large bowl, combine the mayonnaise, lemon juice, soy sauce, wasabi, remaining ¼ teaspoon salt, and the black pepper.

3 Add the pasta, shrimp, avocado, tomatoes, and parsley, and mix.

4 Place the baby spinach on the bottom of the bento box and top with the pasta salad.

PLAN AHEAD

1 Combine the dressing ingredients, halve the grape tomatoes, and chop the parsley the night before. Refrigerate. You can also make the Fresh Fruits Jelly and refrigerate overnight.
2 In the morning, make the Shrimp Avocado Pasta Salad.

COLD SOMEN NOODLE BENTO

Somen noodles are thin noodles that are available in dried form and often eaten cold with a dipping sauce. Somen has a nice, smooth texture and cooks fast. Eaten by itself, it can be light fare, but you can make it a more satisfying meal by serving it with eggs and vegetables. Dip the noodles in the sauce as you eat or pour the sauce over the noodles.

TO MAKE THIS BENTO

Each bento has a main-dish recipe (below), side-dish recipes (page 163), and additional ingredients.

Somen (see recipe below)

PREP TIME: 15 MINUTES   **COOK TIME:** 10 MINUTES   **YIELD:** 2 SERVINGS

SOMEN

2 to 3 bunches (150 to 200 g)
    dried somen noodles
2 teaspoons grated ginger
1 green onion, chopped
2 tablespoons (30 ml)
    Mentsuyu (page 204)
¼ cup (60 ml) water
Kinshi Tamago (page 194),
    for garnish
Sweet and Salty Shiitake
    Mushrooms (page 190),
    for garnish
4 thin slices ham, for garnish
1 small cucumber, julienned,
    for garnish
2 shiso leaves (or lettuce, if not
    available), for garnish

1 Bring a medium saucepan of water to a boil. Add the somen noodles and cook for 2 minutes, then drain. Rinse the noodles under running water, rubbing them together as you do so.

2 While the somen are loose and soft, take a small bunch and roll them around your finger to make a small bird's nest. Make 10 to 12 noodle nests (per person) and put them in a bento box. Top with the grated ginger and chopped green onion.

3 Mix the mentsuyu and ¼ cup (60 ml) water for a dipping sauce.

4 Garnish with the Kinshi Tamago, Sweet and Salty Shiitake Mushrooms, ham, cucumber, and shiso leaves.

PLAN AHEAD

1 Mentsuyu can be made in advance and kept in an airtight container in the refrigerator for up to 2 to 3 weeks.
2 Make the Kinshi Tamago and Sweet and Salty Shiitake Mushrooms the night before. Also julienne the cucumber.
3 In the morning, cook the Somen and pack it in bite-size bunches so that the noodles are easier to eat. Add the garnishes.

POPULAR JAPANESE BENTO

CHICKEN KARAAGE BENTO

Karaage, or fried chicken, is one of the most popular main dishes for bento in Japan. Marinated bite-size chicken pieces are lightly coated with seasoned flour and starch before being fried, which gives it a perfectly crispy texture on the outside. Karaage makes for a great appetizer, a dinner main, or a perfect portion for your lunch bento.

TO MAKE THIS BENTO

Each bento has a main-dish recipe (below), side-dish recipes (page 163), and additional ingredients.

Chicken Karaage (see recipe below)
Steamed Rice (page 18), with furikake of choice
Green Beans and Tomato Salad (page 178)

1 hard-boiled egg
1 or 2 large lettuce leaves

PREP TIME: 15 MINUTES   **COOK TIME:** 10 MINUTES   **YIELD:** 2 SERVINGS

CHICKEN KARAAGE

2 boneless, skinless chicken thighs, cut into bite-size pieces
1 tablespoon (15 ml) sake
2 teaspoons soy sauce
¼ teaspoon salt, divided
1 teaspoon grated fresh ginger
¼ cup (30 g) all-purpose flour
¼ cup (24 g) cornstarch
Black pepper, to taste
Vegetable oil, for frying

1 In a medium bowl, combine the chicken with the sake, soy sauce, half of the salt, and the ginger. Let the chicken marinate for 10 minutes.

2 In a separate medium bowl, combine the flour, cornstarch, remaining salt, and black pepper. Dredge the marinated chicken pieces in the flour mixture.

3 Heat the oil in a large saucepan over medium-high heat (350°F, or 180°C). Fry the chicken for 5 to 6 minutes, or until cooked through. Remove from the pan with a slotted spoon and place on a paper towel–lined plate to absorb excess oil.

PLAN AHEAD

1 Enjoy Karaage and Green Beans and Tomato Salad for dinner, and have leftovers in tomorrow's bento. Reserve some chicken thighs, marinate overnight, and fry the Karaage in the morning.

2 Before you go to bed, hard-boil the egg and set the timer on the rice cooker.

3 In the morning, fry or reheat the Karaage in a toaster or conventional oven.

HAMBURGER STEAK BENTO

Hamburger steak is a popular entrée in Japan that falls somewhere between a hamburger patty and meatloaf. A fifty-fifty ratio of beef and pork makes the dish more flavorful and tender. If you want to make this for dinner and include in tomorrow's bento, leave some raw-meat mixture to cook in the morning.

TO MAKE THIS BENTO

Each bento has a main-dish recipe (below), side-dish recipes (page 163), and additional ingredients.

Hamburger Steak (see recipe below)
Steamed Rice (page 18), with Noritama Furikake (page 125)
Potato Salad (page 180)

4 blanched broccoli florets
6 cherry tomatoes
2 lettuce leaves

PREP TIME: 10 MINUTES   **COOK TIME:** 10 MINUTES   **YIELD:** 2 SERVINGS

HAMBURGER STEAK

2 tablespoons (30 g) ketchup
2 tablespoons (30 ml) Worcestershire sauce
3 tablespoons (21 g) bread crumbs (preferably panko)
1 tablespoon (15 ml) milk
¼ pound (113 g) ground beef
¼ pound (113 g) ground pork
½ large egg, beaten
¼ medium onion, minced
⅛ teaspoon salt
White pepper, to taste
1 teaspoon vegetable oil
1 tablespoon (15 ml) sake

1   Combine the ketchup and Worcestershire sauce in a small bowl. Set aside.

2   Combine the bread crumbs and milk in a large bowl. Add the beef, pork, egg, onion, salt, and pepper, and mix well.

3   Divide the mixture into 6 equal pieces and roll into oval balls. Push down to shape the balls into ½-inch-thick (13 mm) oval patties with ⅓-inch (8 mm) indentations in the middle.

4   Heat the oil in a large skillet over medium heat, add the patties, and cook for 3 minutes on one side. Flip, cover, and cook for another 3 minutes, or until cooked through. Add the sake to the pan, and then stir in the sauce. Cook for 30 seconds, coating the steaks with sauce.

PLAN AHEAD

1   Enjoy Hamburger Steak and Potato Salad for dinner, and have leftovers in tomorrow's bento.
2   Before you go to bed, blanch the broccoli and set the timer on the rice cooker.
3   In the morning, cook the Hamburger Steak.

YAKINIKU BENTO

Yakiniku beef is usually cooked on a special griddle, electric or charcoal, and dipped in a garlicky yakiniku sauce. Our simplified Yakiniku is cooked with the sauce in a skillet. The beef can be loin or chuck, or short rib if you like a fattier meat. Yakiniku sauce is available bottled at Japanese markets for convenience; however, our sauce is quick to make. Also, you can make a smaller amount or use leftover sauce on chicken and stir-fried vegetables.

TO MAKE THIS BENTO

Each bento has a main-dish recipe (below), side-dish recipes (page 163), and additional ingredients.

Yakiniku (see recipe below)
Steamed Rice (page 18), with umeboshi
   (pickled sour plum)

Pan-Fried Kabocha (page 176)
Cucumber and Seaweed Sunomono (page 202)
2 butter lettuce leaves

PREP TIME: 10 MINUTES   **COOK TIME:** 5 MINUTES   **YIELD:** 2 SERVINGS

YAKINIKU

YAKINIKU SAUCE
1 dried chile pepper, seeded
   and sliced
¼ cup (60 ml) soy sauce
2 tablespoons (30 ml) sugar
2 tablespoons (30 ml) mirin
1 teaspoon grated ginger
1 teaspoon grated garlic
1½ teaspoons sesame seeds
1½ teaspoons ground
   sesame seeds
1½ teaspoons sesame oil

BEEF
1 teaspoon vegetable oil
5 ounces (150 g) beef, thinly
   sliced (¼ inch, or 6 mm
   thick)

1 **To make the yakiniku sauce:** In a small saucepan, bring all the sauce ingredients to a boil and let the sauce boil for 1 minute. Cool and store in a clean airtight container.

2 **To make the beef:** Heat the oil in a large skillet over medium heat. Sear the beef for about 1 minute per side (depending on the thickness of the meat), then add 2 to 3 tablespoons (30 to 45 ml) of Yakiniku Sauce and stir to coat. Remove from the heat.

PLAN AHEAD

1 The Yakiniku Sauce can be made in advance and stored in an airtight container in the refrigerator for up to 2 weeks.
2 The Cucumber and Seaweed Sunomono can be made the night before.
3 Before you go to bed, set the timer on the rice cooker.
4 In the morning, while cooking the beef, make the Pan-Fried Kabocha in a different pan.

OKONOMIYAKI BENTO

Okonomiyaki is a savory cabbage pancake with okonomiyaki sauce and Japanese mayo. The batter has *nagaimo* (Chinese yam), which gives the pancake a softer texture and helps it taste good even at room temperature, but you can omit it if you can't find it.

TO MAKE THIS BENTO

Each bento has a main-dish recipe (below), side-dish recipes (page 163), and additional ingredients.

Okonomiyaki (see recipe below)
Tomato and Onion Salad (page 178)

Green salad with strawberries and Cheddar cheese
Dressing of choice

PREP TIME: 15 MINUTES   **COOK TIME:** 10 MINUTES   **YIELD:** 2 SERVINGS

OKONOMIYAKI

3 ounces (100 g) pork belly,
 thinly sliced
1 cup (120 g) all-purpose flour
1 cup (235 ml) Dashi (page XX)
1 large egg
2 tablespoons (20 g) grated
 nagaimo (Chinese yam)
¼ teaspoon salt
¼ teaspoon soy sauce
3 cups (270 g) finely chopped
 cabbage
4 green onions, finely chopped
2 tablespoons (20 g) finely
 chopped benishoga (pickled
 red ginger)
1 tablespoon (15 ml) vegetable
 oil
Okonomiyaki sauce, for topping
Japanese mayonnaise, for topping
Aonori (dried green seaweed
 flakes), for topping
Katsuobushi (dried bonito flakes),
 for topping

1 Cut the sliced pork into 1-inch-wide (2.5 cm) pieces.

2 In a large bowl, whisk together the flour, dashi, egg, nagaimo, salt, and soy sauce until smooth. Add the chopped cabbage, green onions, and benishoga and combine well.

3 Heat the oil in a large skillet over medium heat. Pour one-quarter of the batter into a 4-inch (10 cm) circle. Top with one-quarter of the pork slices. (You can cook 4 pancakes in the pan at once, but if the pan is too crowded, cook 2 at a time.) Cook until the pancake bottom turns golden brown, 3 to 4 minutes. Flip and cook the other side until the pork becomes crispy, another 3 to 4 minutes.

4 Flip the pancake one more time. With the pork side up, spread the okonomiyaki sauce and mayo on the pancake. Sprinkle with aonori and katsuobushi.

PLAN AHEAD

1 Prepare the batter and cut up the cabbage, green onions, and benishoga the night before, but don't combine them together.
2 In the morning, while cooking the Okonomiyaki, quickly fix the Tomato and Onion Salad and green salad.

KOROKKE BENTO

Korokke is the Japanese adaptation of the French croquette. You can pick up delicious korokke at deli counters everywhere in Japan. This homemade version is tasty and irresistible.

TO MAKE THIS BENTO

Each bento has a main-dish recipe (below), side-dish recipes (page 163), and additional ingredients.

Korokke (see recipe below)
Steamed Rice (page 18)
Coleslaw (page 183)

Tamagoyaki with Spinach (page 22)
Grape tomatoes

PREP TIME: 20 MINUTES   **COOK TIME:** 20 MINUTES   **YIELD:** 2 SERVINGS

KOROKKE

1 medium russet potato, cut
   into 2-inch (5 cm) pieces
½ teaspoon vegetable oil, plus
   more for frying
¼ pound (113 g) ground beef
¼ medium onion, minced
¼ teaspoon salt, plus more to
   taste
Pinch black pepper, plus more
   to taste
2 tablespoons (30 ml)
   all-purpose flour
1 large egg
1 cup (50 g) panko
Tonkatsu sauce,
   Worcestershire sauce,
   or ketchup, for drizzling or
   dipping (optional)

1 Boil the potato until soft, about 10 minutes. Drain, transfer to a medium bowl, and mash.

2 Heat ½ teaspoon of the oil in a skillet over medium-high heat. Add the ground beef and cook until browned. Add the onion and cook for another 3 minutes. Season with the salt and pepper.

3 Combine the beef mixture and mashed potato. Season with more salt and pepper if needed. Scoop the mixture in heaping tablespoons, form into 6 to 8 balls, and flatten a bit. Place on a plate and refrigerate for 10 minutes. Coat the patties in the flour, followed by the egg and then the panko. Heat 2 inches (5 cm) of oil in a large saucepan over medium-high heat (350°F, or 180°C). Fry for 3 to 4 minutes per side.

PLAN AHEAD

1 Enjoy Korokke and Coleslaw for dinner, and have leftovers for tomorrow's bento.
2 Before you go to bed, set the timer on the rice cooker.
3 In the morning, make the Tamagoyaki and reheat the Korokke in a toaster or conventional oven. Alternatively, you can freeze the breaded but uncooked Korokke and fry straight from the freezer.

SWEET AND SOUR MEATBALLS BENTO

There are many variations of meatballs in the world, but this is certainly one of the best. Homemade pork meatballs are fried and coated in a thick sweet and sour sauce. The sauce has the perfect balance of those flavours.

TO MAKE THIS BENTO

Each bento has a main-dish recipe (below), side-dish recipes (page 163), and additional ingredients.

Sweet and Sour Meatballs (see recipe below)
Steamed Rice (page 18)
Potato Salad (page 180)

Carrot Namul (page 166)
Grape tomatoes

PREP TIME: 15 MINUTES   **COOK TIME:** 15 MINUTES   **YIELD:** 2 SERVINGS

SWEET AND SOUR MEATBALLS

MEATBALLS
½ pound (227 g) ground pork
½ medium onion, minced
1 large egg
2 tablespoons (6 g) panko
1 tablespoon (15 ml) cornstarch
1 teaspoon grated fresh ginger
1 teaspoon soy sauce
1 teaspoon sesame oil
¼ teaspoon salt
Vegetable oil, for frying

SAUCE
¼ cup (60 ml) water
2 tablespoons (30 ml) soy sauce
3 tablespoons (45 ml) vinegar
2 tablespoons (30 ml) sugar
2 tablespoons (30 ml) sake
2 teaspoons cornstarch

1 **To make the meatballs:** In a large bowl, combine all the meatball ingredients except the oil for frying. Shape the mixture into bite-size (1 inch, or 2.5 cm) balls.

2 Heat 1 inch (2.5 cm) of oil in a large saucepan over medium-high heat (350°F, or 180ºC). Fry the meatballs for 5 minutes, or until browned.

3 **To make the sauce:** In a medium skillet, add all the sauce ingredients. Heat until thickened, stirring constantly. Add the meatballs and coat them with the sauce.

PLAN AHEAD

1 The meatballs and sauce can be cooked ahead of time and kept in the freezer for up to 2 weeks.
2 Make the Potato Salad and Carrot Namul the day before.
3 Before you go to bed, set the timer on the rice cooker.
4 In the morning, reheat the Sweet and Sour Meatballs in the microwave.

CHICKEN NUGGETS BENTO

Instead of stocking your freezer with store-bought versions, make these healthy and tasty chicken nuggets. You can make these nuggets in advance and freeze them. Keep baked or unbaked nuggets frozen for up to 1 month. If freezing before baking, place them on a baking sheet, freeze for 1 hour, and store them in a freezer bag; if freezing after baking, make sure to completely cool the nuggets before freezing.

TO MAKE THIS BENTO

Each bento has a main-dish recipe (below), side-dish recipes (page 163), and additional ingredients.

Baked Chicken Nuggets (see recipe below)
Steamed Rice (page 18), with furikake of choice
Tamagoyaki with Green Onions (page 22)
Broccoli Namul (page 168)

1 or 2 mini sweet peppers
1 large lettuce leaf
Ketchup (optional)

PREP TIME: 10 MINUTES   **COOK TIME:** 15 MINUTES   **YIELD:** 2 SERVINGS

BAKED CHICKEN NUGGETS

½ pound (227 g) chicken tenderloins
½ teaspoon garlic powder
¼ teaspoon salt
¼ teaspoon black pepper
1 tablespoon (15 ml) all-purpose flour
1 large egg, beaten
1 tablespoon (15 ml) vegetable oil
⅓ cup (17 g) panko
1 tablespoon (15 ml) cornmeal

1 Preheat the oven to 425°F (220°C).

2 Cut each chicken tenderloin into 2 or 3 pieces. Sprinkle the chicken with the garlic powder, salt, and pepper, and then dredge lightly in the flour.

3 Whisk together the beaten egg and oil in a shallow dish. Mix together the panko and cornmeal in another dish. Dip each chicken piece into the egg mixture and then into the panko mixture. Place on a baking sheet.

4 Bake for 15 minutes (20 to 25 minutes if frozen), or until the chicken is cooked through.

PLAN AHEAD

1 Enjoy Chicken Nuggets for dinner or freeze them in advance.
2 Before you go to bed, make the Broccoli Namul and set the timer on the rice cooker.
3 In the morning, reheat or cook the nuggets in the oven and make the Tamagoyaki.

10-MINUTE BENTO

COLD SHABU SHABU SALAD BENTO

Shabu shabu is a Japanese hot-pot dish that is very popular during the winter. Paper-thin meat is cooked in a hot pot, usually at the dinner table. During the hot summer months or on busy weekdays, you can still enjoy the shabu shabu meat without the hassle of setting up a hot pot. Pork sliced paper-thin can be cooked almost instantly in boiling water on the stove. It is a great way to add protein to a salad.

TO MAKE THIS BENTO

Each bento has a main-dish recipe (below), side-dish recipes (page 163), and additional ingredients.

Cold Shabu Shabu Salad (see recipe below)

PREP TIME: 7 MINUTES   **COOK TIME:** 3 MINUTES   **YIELD:** 2 SERVINGS

COLD SHABU SHABU SALAD

2 tablespoons (30 ml) soy sauce

2 tablespoons (30 ml) rice vinegar

1 tablespoon (15 ml) sesame oil

2 ounces (60 g) harusame (dried bean thread noodles)

½ pound (227 g) pork loin, very thinly sliced

2 cups (40 g) chopped romaine lettuce

2 radishes, thinly sliced

1 green onion, chopped

1 Bring water to a boil water in 2 medium saucepans, one for the harusame and the other for the pork.

2 In a small bowl, mix together the soy sauce, rice vinegar, and sesame oil, and divide into 2 dressing containers with lids.

3 When the water boils, cook the harusame for 2 to 3 minutes, or according to the package directions. Drain and let cool.

4 In the other saucepan, drop the pork slices, one by one, into the boiling water and cook for 15 seconds, or until cooked. Remove the pork from the hot water, place in ice water to cool, and pat dry with a paper towel.

5 In a bento box, place the lettuce, harusame, pork, radishes, and green onions. Pour the dressing on top right before eating.

PLAN AHEAD

1 Prep the lettuce, radishes, and green onion, along with the dressing, the night before

2 In the morning, cook the harusame and pork.

HOT DOG BENTO

Hot dogs are one of Americans' all-time favorite foods, but here we've introduced a twist by adding cooked cabbage seasoned with curry powder and vinegar. This cabbage with a little spice gives extra flavor and nutrition to the classic dish. If you prefer, you can the boil the hot dogs instead of frying.

TO MAKE THIS BENTO

Each bento has a main-dish recipe (below), side-dish recipes (page 163), and additional ingredients.

Hot Dog with Curry-Flavored Cabbage (see recipe below)

Yogurt with dried fruits and nuts

4 large lettuce leaves

4 cherry tomatoes

PREP TIME: 3 MINUTES   COOK TIME: 7 MINUTES   YIELD: 2 SERVINGS

HOT DOG WITH CURRY-FLAVORED CABBAGE

2 hot dogs (or any sausages)
2 teaspoons vegetable oil, divided
1 cup (70 g) shredded cabbage
¼ cup (30 g) thinly sliced onion (optional)
Pinch curry powder
Pinch salt
½ teaspoon apple cider vinegar
1 teaspoon water
2 hot dog buns
Ketchup, for topping (optional)
Mustard, for topping (optional)

1 Make diagonal cuts on the surface of the hot dogs. In a medium skillet, heat 1 teaspoon of the oil over medium heat. Add the hot dogs, cover, and cook for 5 to 6 minutes, turning a few times.

2 While the hot dogs are cooking, in a separate medium skillet, heat the remaining 1 teaspoon oil over medium heat. Add the cabbage and onion (if using), and cook for 1 minute. Add the curry powder, salt, vinegar, and water, and cook for a few more minutes.

3 Put half of the curried cabbage in a bun and place a hot dog on top of the cabbage. Repeat with the remaining bun, cabbage, and hot dog. Drizzle with ketchup and mustard, if desired.

PLAN AHEAD

1 A little prep the night before, such as cutting up the vegetables (or using already-shredded cabbage), will free your time in the morning.
2 In the morning, cook the hot dogs, making sure to cover them with a lid to heat quicker. But check often so they don't burn.

QUESADILLA BENTO

A quesadilla is a grilled tortilla with melted cheese inside. It is one of the most-beloved Mexican foods, especially among children. While cheese alone in a quesadilla can be quite tasty (and kids love it that way!), you can also add some protein and/or vegetables, such as cooked chicken pieces, beans, tomatoes, and onions. The additional black bean and corn salad goes well with the quesadilla, and it's easy to make.

TO MAKE THIS BENTO

Each bento has a main-dish recipe (below), side-dish recipes (page 163), and additional ingredients.

Cheese Quesadilla (see recipe below)
Black Bean and Corn Salad (see recipe below)

Seasonal fruit

PREP TIME: 4 MINUTES   **COOK TIME:** 6 MINUTES   **YIELD:** 2 SERVINGS

CHEESE QUESADILLA AND BLACK BEAN AND CORN SALAD

BLACK BEAN AND CORN SALAD
1 can (15 ounces, or 425 g) black beans, rinsed and drained
1 can (15 ounces, or 425 g) whole kernel corn, drained
¼ medium red bell pepper, chopped
¼ cup (15 g) chopped cilantro
1 lime, juiced
½ teaspoon salt
¼ teaspoon ground cumin
Black pepper, to taste

CHEESE QUESADILLA
2 large flour tortillas
1 cup (115 g) shredded cheese (Cheddar, Monterey Jack, or Mexican blend)

1 **To make the black bean and corn salad:** Combine all the salad ingredients in a bowl. Set aside.

2 **To make the cheese quesadilla:** Heat a large skillet over medium-high heat. Place a tortilla in the pan and cook for 30 seconds. Flip and top with half the cheese on one-half of the tortilla. Fold in half and cook for 1 minute, or until the bottom is brown. Flip and cook for another minute. Repeat to make the second quesadilla.

3 Cut each quesadilla into 4 pieces.

PLAN AHEAD

1 The Black Bean and Corn Salad can be made the night before.
2 In the morning, make the Cheese Quesadilla.

PINWHEEL SANDWICHES BENTO

If you are a busy parent with small children and are tired of packing the same old sandwich for lunch, try pinwheel sandwiches. They have the familiar ingredients that kids love, such as ham and PB&J, but with a different look! Try to find sandwich bread that is larger and thinner, to make it easier to roll. If the slice of bread is too stiff, flatten it a bit using a rolling pin, or microwave for a few seconds.

TO MAKE THIS BENTO

Each bento has a main-dish recipe (below), side-dish recipes (page 163), and additional ingredients.

Ham and Lettuce Pinwheel Sandwiches (see recipe below)

Peanut Butter and Jelly Pinwheel Sandwiches (see recipe below)

PREP TIME: 10 MINUTES   YIELD: 2 SERVINGS

PINWHEEL SANDWICHES

6 slices large sandwich bread, crusts removed, divided

HAM AND LETTUCE
Mayonnaise, to taste (optional)
3 green lettuce leaves
3 slices ham

PB&J
Peanut butter, to taste
Jam of choice, to taste

1 Place each of the 6 slices of bread on its own sheet of plastic wrap.

2 **To make the ham and lettuce sandwich:** Spread mayonnaise (if using) on 3 slices of bread and top each slice with a lettuce leaf and a slice of ham.

3 **To make the PB&J:** Spread the peanut butter and jam on the remaining 3 slices of bread.

4 Roll each bread slice from one side to the other and immediately wrap with the plastic wrap. Squeeze and twist both sides of plastic wrap to hold its shape.

5 Cut diagonally in half over the plastic wrap.

PLAN AHEAD

Pinwheel sandwiches can be made the night before, wrapped, and refrigerated. Wait to cut in half in the morning.

YAKISOBA BENTO

Yakisoba is stir-fried noodles with meat and vegetables seasoned with yakisoba sauce, which is similar to Worcestershire sauce. It is usually topped with *aonori* (dried green seaweed flakes) and *benishoga* (pickled red ginger). Yakisoba noodles are sold at Japanese or Asian markets in the refrigerated section, and often come with packets of powdered "sauce." You can use that or bottled yakisoba sauce, also available at Japanese markets.

TO MAKE THIS BENTO

Each bento has a main-dish recipe (below), side-dish recipes (page 163), and additional ingredients.

Yakisoba (see recipe below)

8 to 10 grape tomatoes

6 cucumber slices

2 lettuce leaves

PREP TIME: 2 MINUTES   **COOK TIME:** 8 MINUTES   **YIELD:** 2 SERVINGS

YAKISOBA

1 tablespoon (15 ml) vegetable oil

¼ pound (113 g) ground pork

½ cup (60 g) shredded carrot

1 cup (50 g) bean sprouts

3 green onions, cut into 2-inch-long (5 cm) pieces

2 packages (5.3 oz, or 150g, each) yakisoba noodles

¼ cup (60 ml) water

Salt and black pepper, to taste

¼ cup (60 ml) yakisoba sauce

Aonori (dried green seaweed flakes), for topping

Benishoga (pickled red ginger), for topping

1 Heat the oil in a medium nonstick skillet over medium heat. Add the ground pork and cook for 1 minute, stirring a couple times.

2 Add the carrot, bean sprouts, and green onions, and stir for a few seconds. Add the noodles and water, cover, and steam for 1 minute.

3 Loosen the noodles, season them with a little salt and pepper, and stir in the yakisoba sauce. Stir-fry for 30 seconds, or until any remaining liquid is gone. Remove from the heat.

4 Top with the aonori and benishoga.

PLAN AHEAD

In the morning, while making the Yakisoba, wash and cut the veggies.

PIZZA BENTO

English muffin pizza is a quick and easy comfort food for children and grown-ups alike. The muffin halves can fit in most bento boxes without the need to cut into slices. Lightly toasting the muffins before spreading the sauce is recommended for a crunchier crust, but you can skip this step if you like a softer crust or want to cut the prep time. The additional spinach and strawberry salad can be prepared in no time at all. Use good-quality extra-virgin olive oil and aged balsamic vinegar if possible. The sweetness of the aged balsamic vinegar pairs well with strawberries.

TO MAKE THIS BENTO

Each bento has a main-dish recipe (below), side-dish recipes (page 163), and additional ingredients.

English Muffin Pizza (see recipe below)   Spinach and Strawberry Salad (see recipe below)

PREP TIME: 5 MINUTES   **COOK TIME:** 5 MINUTES   **YIELD:** 2 SERVINGS

ENGLISH MUFFIN PIZZA AND SPINACH AND STRAWBERRY SALAD

ENGLISH MUFFIN PIZZA
2 English muffins, split
¼ cup (60 g) store-bought pizza or marinara sauce
½ cup (58 g) shredded mozzarella cheese
Mini pepperoni or topping of choice, to taste

SPINACH AND STRAWBERRY SALAD
4 to 6 strawberries
1 cup (20 g) baby spinach
1 tablespoon (15 ml) extra-virgin olive oil
1 teaspoon aged balsamic vinegar
Pinch salt

1 To make the English muffin pizza: Preheat the oven to 450°F (230°C), or you can use a toaster oven. If you wish, lightly toast the English muffins for 2 to 3 minutes.

2 Place the muffin halves, cut side up, on a baking sheet, and top with the sauce, cheese, and pepperoni. Bake for 5 minutes, or until the cheese is melted. Prepare the salad while the pizza cooks.

3 To make the spinach and strawberry salad: Hull and thinly slice the strawberries and place them on top of the baby spinach in a bento box.

4 In a small container with a lid, mix together the olive oil, vinegar, and salt, and pack on the side.

PLAN AHEAD

1 Although you can easily whip up the salad while the pizza is in the oven, the Spinach and Strawberry Salad can be made the night before.
2 In the morning, prep and bake the English Muffin Pizza.

CORN CHOWDER BENTO

This corn chowder is so simple, it takes no time to make in the morning. Pack it in an insulated thermal jar so that it will stay warm until lunchtime. In order to cut the cooking time, we used Canadian bacon here, but if you are cooking regular bacon for breakfast anyway, add the cooked bacon and some fat for a richer flavor.

TO MAKE THIS BENTO

Each bento has a main-dish recipe (below), side-dish recipes (page 163), and additional ingredients.

Quick Corn Chowder (see recipe below)
Crackers

Seasonal fruit

PREP TIME: 2 MINUTES   **COOK TIME:** 8 MINUTES   **YIELD:** 2 SERVINGS

QUICK CORN CHOWDER

1 tablespoon (15 g) unsalted
   butter
½ medium onion, chopped
⅓ medium carrot, diced
1 tablespoon (15 ml) all-purpose
   flour
5 slices Canadian bacon,
   chopped
1 cup (235 ml) chicken broth
1 can (15 ounces, or 425 g) corn
1 can (15 ounces, or 425 g)
   creamed corn
¼ cup (60 ml) half-and-half
¼ teaspoon salt
Black pepper, to taste

1 Melt the butter in a medium saucepan over medium heat. Add the onion and carrot, and cook and stir for 2 minutes.

2 Add the flour and cook for another minute.

3 Add the Canadian bacon, broth, corn, and creamed corn, and bring to a boil over high heat, stirring often. Reduce the heat to medium-low and cook for 3 minutes.

4 Add the half-and-half and season with the salt and pepper.

PLAN AHEAD

1 Make the Quick Corn Chowder the day before and keep it in the refrigerator.
2 In the morning, reheat it in a saucepan and transfer to an insulated jar.

GRANOLA BENTO

Granola is a healthy choice for a light meal because of its high fiber content, along with other nutrients, such as vitamins, minerals, and protein; however, watch out for the amount of a serving. Granola has surprisingly high calories (especially the packaged versions) from fat and sugar. The addition of fresh vegetables and berries makes for a healthier meal. To liven up the veggies, make this easy but tasty green onion dip.

TO MAKE THIS BENTO

Each bento has a main-dish recipe (below), side-dish recipes (page 163), and additional ingredients.

Granola
Milk
Vegetable sticks (20 petite carrots, 2 celery
   stalks, ½ bell pepper)

Green Onion Dip (see recipe below)
Assorted berries

PREP TIME: 3 MINUTES   **YIELD:** 2-PLUS SERVINGS

GREEN ONION DIP

3 green onions, finely chopped
8 ounces (235 g) sour cream
2 tablespoons (15 g) onion soup
   mix
1 teaspoon freshly squeezed
   lemon juice

Combine all the dip ingredients.

PLAN AHEAD

1 To make prep easier, consider using already-cut veggies and a high-quality store-bought granola (though you can make your own homemade granola in advance).
2 Make the Green Onion Dip the day before and refrigerate.
3 In the morning, cut up the veggies if not using already-cut ones.

SPICY CHICKEN WRAP BENTO

These chicken wraps are made with deli rotisserie chicken and require no cooking. Perfect for a busy morning! The chicken pieces are coated with a spicy and flavorful sriracha mayonnaise. The shredded cabbage and bell peppers add a nice crunch.

TO MAKE THIS BENTO

Each bento has a main-dish recipe (below), side-dish recipes (page 163), and additional ingredients.

Spicy Chicken Wrap (see recipe below)

PREP TIME: 10 MINUTES   **YIELD:** 2 SERVINGS

SPICY CHICKEN WRAP

1 tablespoon (15 g) sriracha
1 tablespoon (14 g) mayonnaise
2 to 4 large lettuce leaves
2 large or 4 small flour tortillas
2 cups (220 g) roughly chopped
   cooked chicken
½ cup (35 g) shredded cabbage
¼ medium red bell pepper,
   sliced
Cilantro sprigs, to taste

1 In a medium bowl, combine the sriracha and mayonnaise.

2 Add the chicken pieces to the bowl and stir to coat with the sauce.

3 Place a lettuce leaf on each tortilla, and top with the chicken, shredded cabbage, bell pepper, and cilantro.

4 Tightly roll up each tortilla from the bottom to the top. Wrap with parchment paper, cut in half, and pack in a bento box.

PLAN AHEAD

1 Enjoy rotisserie chicken for dinner, then debone and cut up leftover chicken after dinner.
2 Coat the chicken with the sriracha mayo and cut up the veggies the night before. Keep everything in the refrigerator.
3 In the morning, wrap everything in the tortillas.

BREAKFAST MUFFIN BENTO

A breakfast muffin is the kind of sandwich that you often see at fast-food restaurants and coffee shops: eggs and other fillings between toasted English muffins. It is usually eaten for breakfast, but it works for lunch too. If you are having a typical American breakfast in the morning, make extra eggs and bacon to make this sandwich—it is a quick and easy way to fix your lunch.

TO MAKE THIS BENTO

Each bento has a main-dish recipe (below), side-dish recipes (page 163), and additional ingredients.

Breakfast Muffin (see recipe below)
Red plum or other seasonal fruits

Ketchup (optional)

PREP TIME: 2 MINUTES   **COOK TIME:** 8 MINUTES   **YIELD:** 2 SERVINGS

BREAKFAST MUFFIN

2 slices Cheddar cheese
2 English muffins, split
1 teaspoon vegetable oil, divided
2 to 4 slices Canadian bacon
½ teaspoon butter
2 large eggs
⅛ teaspoon salt
Pinch black pepper
½ cup (10 g) baby spinach
½ tomato, cut into ½-inch-thick (13 mm) slices
1 cup (33 g) alfalfa sprouts

1 Place a cheese slice on the 2 bottom halves of the English muffins. Lightly toast all 4 muffin halves.

2 Heat ½ teaspoon of the oil in a medium skillet over medium heat. Add the Canadian bacon and cook, turning a couple times.

3 While the bacon is cooking, in a small skillet, heat the remaining ½ teaspoon oil and the butter over medium heat and make scrambled eggs. Season with the salt and pepper.

4 On each toasted muffin bottom half with cheese, put half of the scrambled eggs, bacon slice(s), spinach, tomato, and alfalfa sprouts. Top with the other muffin halves.

PLAN AHEAD

Choose vegetables that are already cut or that don't need too much prep (such as baby spinach) to save time when making your lunch in the morning. Also, it is a good idea to keep your fruits washed (except for berries—they get moldy fast) and in the refrigerator ready to eat.

RICE AND GRAIN BOWL BENTO

OMURICE BENTO

Omurice is fried rice seasoned with ketchup and wrapped in a thin egg crepe. Rice and ketchup may sound like an odd combination, but it tastes more like tomato-flavored pilaf. For a bento box, it's hard to wrap the rice with the egg crepe, so place the egg crepe on top.

TO MAKE THIS BENTO

Each bento has a main-dish recipe (below), side-dish recipes (page 163), and additional ingredients.

Omurice (see recipe below)
Avocado and Chicken Salad (page 195)

Okaka Snap Peas (page 184)
12 cherry tomatoes

PREP TIME: 3 MINUTES   **COOK TIME:** 10 MINUTES   **YIELD:** 2 SERVINGS

OMURICE

1 tablespoon (15 g) butter

2 teaspoons vegetable oil, divided

3 slices ham, cut into ½-inch (13 mm) squares

¼ cup (40 g) chopped yellow onion

2 cups (330 g) Steamed Rice (page 18)

¼ teaspoon salt plus an additional pinch, divided

White pepper, to taste

3 tablespoons (45 g) ketchup, plus more for topping (optional)

2 tablespoons (16 g) frozen green peas

2 large eggs

1 Heat the butter and 1 teaspoon of the oil in a medium skillet over medium heat. Add the ham and onion, and cook for 1 to 2 minutes, or until the onion becomes tender. Add the rice and stir-fry, mixing for 1 minute. Season the rice with ¼ teaspoon of the salt and the pepper. Make room in the pan and add the ketchup apart from the rice. Let the ketchup cook by itself for 30 seconds to reduce. Mix the rice and ketchup together, and stir-fry for 1 to 2 minutes. Stir in the frozen peas. Remove from the heat.

2 Beat the eggs and the pinch of salt together. Heat ½ teaspoon of the oil in a small nonstick skillet. Pour half of the egg mixture into the hot pan and make a thin egg crepe. Remove and repeat with the remaining ½ teaspoon oil and egg mixture.

3 Divide the rice in half, and pack in the bento box. Place an egg crepe, cooked side up, over each portion of rice. Squeeze some ketchup (if using) on the egg crepes.

PLAN AHEAD

1 Make the Avocado and Chicken Salad and Okaka Snap Peas the day before.

2 Before you go to bed, set the timer on the rice cooker.

3 In the morning, make the Omurice.

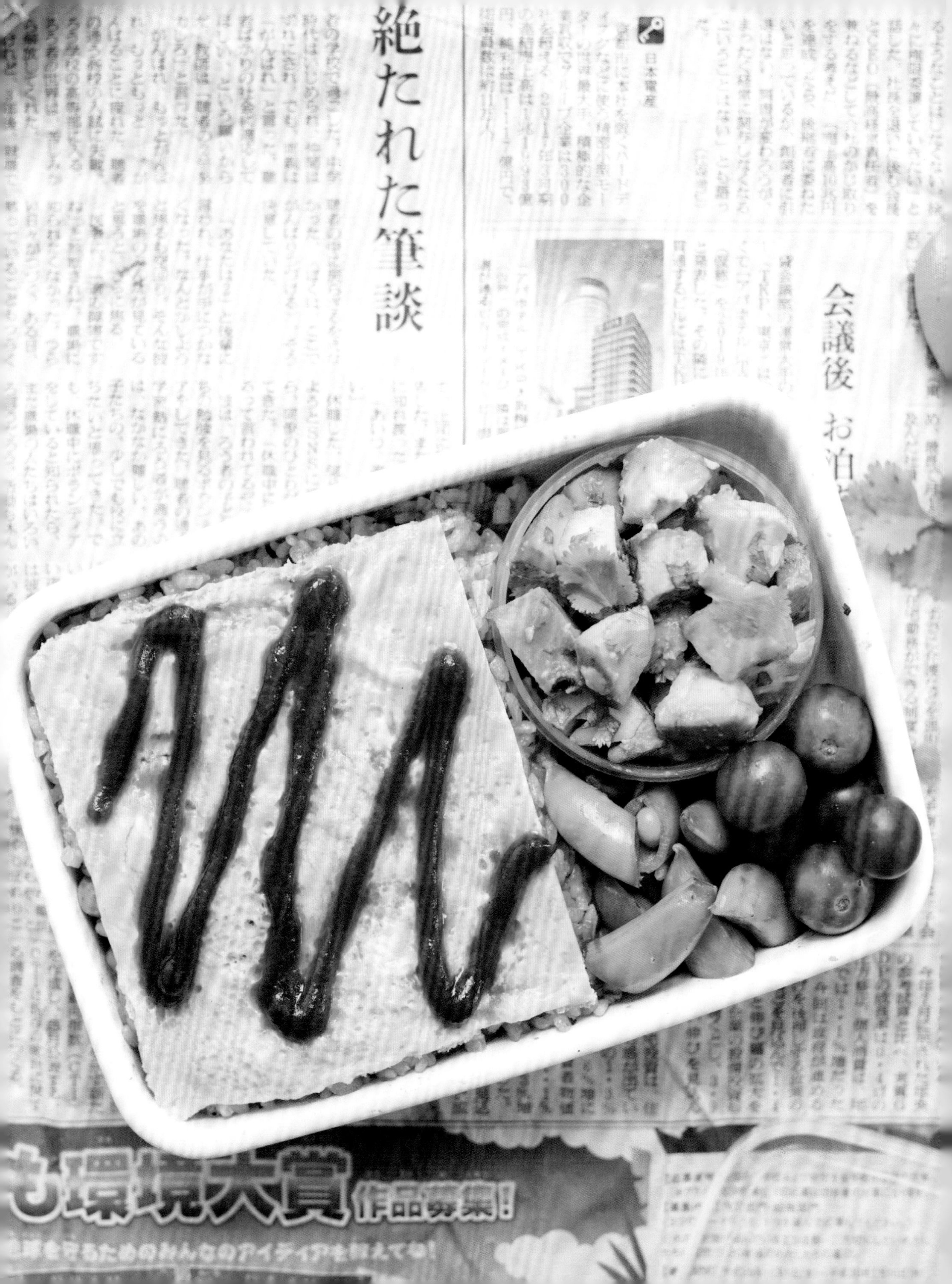
絶たれた筆談
会議後
環境大賞
作品募集!

CHICKEN SOBORO BENTO

Chicken soboro is cooked ground chicken flavored with soy sauce and some sweeteners. It is often served over steamed rice, with finely scrambled eggs and snow peas or green beans. As soboro can be made ahead and kept in the refrigerator for a few days, it is a perfect bento dish.

TO MAKE THIS BENTO

Each bento has a main-dish recipe (below), side-dish recipes (page 163), and additional ingredients.

Chicken Soboro (see recipe below)
Celery Sunomono (page 202)

Tuna and Broccoli Salad (page 186)
6 cherry tomatoes

PREP TIME: TK   **COOK TIME:** 20 MINUTES   **YIELD:** 2 SERVINGS

CHICKEN SOBORO

5 ounces (150 g) ground chicken

2½ teaspoons sugar, divided

1½ tablespoons (23 ml) plus dash soy sauce, divided

1 tablespoon (15 ml) mirin

1½ teaspoons sake

2 large eggs, beaten

Pinch salt

2 cups (330 g) Steamed Rice (page 18)

20 snow peas, blanched and thinly sliced

2 teaspoons chopped benishoga (pickled red ginger), for garnish

1 In a medium saucepan, combine the ground chicken, 1½ teaspoons of the sugar, 1½ tablespoons (23 ml) of the soy sauce, the mirin, and sake. Cook the chicken over medium heat, stirring constantly with a wooden spatula and breaking up the meat, until the sauce has evaporated.

2 In a small nonstick skillet, combine the eggs, the remaining 1 teaspoon sugar, salt, and the remaining dash soy sauce. Cook over medium-low heat, stirring constantly with a wooden spatula, until cooked through but not too dry.

3 Divide the rice between 2 bento boxes, flattening the surface of the rice. Top each with half of the chicken, eggs, and snow peas. Garnish with the benishoga.

PLAN AHEAD

1 Enjoy Chicken Soboro, Celery Sunomono, and Tuna and Broccoli Salad for dinner, and have leftovers in tomorrow's bento.

2 Set the timer on the rice cooker before you go to bed.

3 In the morning, reheat the Chicken Soboro and neatly assemble all the components.

OYAKODON BENTO

Oyakodon is chicken and egg cooked in a sweet and salty sauce that is served over steamed rice. It is a staple lunch dish served at many restaurants in Japan, but it can be easily re-created at home. If you have Mentsuyu (page 204) on hand, seasoning this dish is a breeze. (See the photo for this bento on page 104.)

TO MAKE THIS BENTO

Each bento has a main-dish recipe (below), side-dish recipes (page 163), and additional ingredients.

Oyakodon (see recipe below)
Green Beans with Sesame Sauce (page 169)

Pickled Daikon Radish (page 200)
Red plum or other seasonal fruits

PREP TIME: 5 MINUTES   COOK TIME: 10 MINUTES   YIELD: 2 SERVINGS

OYAKODON

¼ cup (60 ml) Mentsuyu
  (page 204)
1 teaspoon sugar
¼ cup (60 ml) water
½ medium yellow onion, thinly
  sliced
1 chicken breast or thigh
  (about 5 ounces, or 150 g),
  cut into thin, bite-size pieces
2 large eggs
2 cups (330 g) Steamed Rice
  (page 18)
1 green onion, finely chopped, for
  garnish
Shredded nori (roasted
  seaweed), for garnish

1 In a medium saucepan over medium heat, bring the mentsuyu, sugar, and water to a boil.

2 Add the onion slices to the sauce and cook for 1 minute. Add the chicken pieces and cook for a couple minutes, turning once.

3 Beat the eggs in a small bowl and pour over the chicken and onion slices. Cover and cook for 1 minute (traditionally, the eggs in this dish are soft, but you can cook them to your preferred doneness).

4 Slide the egg mixture over the rice. Sprinkle with the chopped green onion and shredded nori.

PLAN AHEAD

1 Make the Green Beans with Sesame Sauce and Pickled Daikon Radish the day before.
2 The Oyakodon topping also can be made through step 2 the night before, but do not put over the rice yet. Alternatively, if you're planning on making the Oyakodon quickly in the morning, make sure you have Mentsuyu in the refrigerator.
3 Before you go to bed, set the timer on the rice cooker.
4 In the morning, cook the Oyakodon.

GYUDON BENTO

Gyudon (beef bowl) is a comfort food prepared at home and also served at restaurants across Japan. Thinly sliced beef and onion are seasoned in a sweet and salty broth and piled on top of steamed rice. This hearty rice bowl is quite satisfying, even for teenagers and young adults with a big appetite.

> ## TO MAKE THIS BENTO
> Each bento has a main-dish recipe (below), side-dish recipes (page 163), and additional ingredients.
>
> **Gyudon (see recipe below)**   **Apple, sliced**
> **Cauliflower and Snow Pea Salad (page 181)**

PREP TIME: 5 MINUTES   **COOK TIME:** 15 MINUTES   **YIELD:** 2 SERVINGS

GYUDON

1 cup (235 ml) Dashi (page 20)
1 medium onion, thinly sliced
¼ cup (60 ml) soy sauce
3 tablespoons (38 g) sugar
2 tablespoons (30 ml) sake
½ pound (227 g) beef, thinly
  sliced and cut into 2-inch-wide
  (5 cm) strips
1 teaspoon grated fresh ginger
Steamed Rice (page 18)
Benishoga (pickled red ginger),
  for garnish

1 Bring the dashi to a boil in a medium saucepan. Add the sliced onion and cook for 3 minutes.

2 Add the soy sauce, sugar, and sake, and cook for 3 more minutes.

3 Add the beef and grated ginger and cook for 5 additional minutes.

4 Pour the meat and sauce over the rice, and top with the benishoga.

PLAN AHEAD

1 Make the sauce for the Gyudon through step 2 and the Cauliflower and Snow Pea Salad the night before.
2 Before you go to bed, set the timer on the rice cooker.
3 In the morning, heat the sauce, cook the beef with the ginger, and pour over the rice.

TACO RICE BENTO

Taco rice is a rice-bowl dish made with taco ingredients, such as seasoned ground beef, shredded lettuce, cheese, and tomato. It was originally created in the Okinawa region of Japan near the US military base there and has gradually become a popular dish throughout Japan. It is similar to a taco salad, but instead of a tortilla bowl, everything is placed on a bed of rice.

TO MAKE THIS BENTO

Each bento has a main-dish recipe (below), side-dish recipes (page 163), and additional ingredients.

Taco Rice (see recipe below)   Seasonal fruits

PREP TIME: 5 MINUTES   **COOK TIME:** 13 MINUTES   **YIELD:** 2 SERVINGS

TACO RICE

1 teaspoon vegetable oil
½ pound (227 g) ground beef
½ medium onion, minced
1 clove garlic, minced
8 ounces (227 g) tomato sauce
1 teaspoon cumin
1 teaspoon paprika
½ teaspoon salt
Black pepper, to taste
Steamed Rice (page 18), at
    room temperature
Lettuce, shredded or cut into
    small pieces
Shredded cheese
Grape tomatoes, halved

1 Heat a large skillet over medium-high heat. Add the oil, followed by the ground beef. Cook until the meat browns, then stir in the onion and garlic. Cook for 3 minutes.

2 Add the tomato sauce, cumin, paprika, salt, and pepper. Lower the heat to medium and cook until the sauce is reduced, about 10 minutes. Remove from the heat and let cool.

3 In a bento box, place the rice and top with the lettuce, meat, cheese, and tomatoes.

PLAN AHEAD

1 Cook the ground beef and prepare the toppings the day before.
2 Before you go to bed, set the timer on the rice cooker.
3 In the morning, assemble the Taco Rice.

QUINOA SALAD BENTO

Quinoa has become a wildly popular grain in the United States because of its health benefits. Quinoa's mild flavor goes well with any kind of flavoring, and here, it is mixed with a red wine vinaigrette. Along with the green beans, pistachios, and dried cranberries, this salad is a satisfying dish for lunch.

TO MAKE THIS BENTO

Each bento has a main-dish recipe (below), side-dish recipes (page 163), and additional ingredients.

Quinoa Salad (see recipe below)
Rotisserie chicken
Green salad with tomatoes and feta cheese

Dressing of choice
Grapes

PREP TIME: 5 MINUTES   **COOK TIME:** 18 MINUTES   **YIELD:** 2 SERVINGS

QUINOA SALAD

½ cup (85 g) dried quinoa
¾ cup (180 ml) chicken broth
10 green beans
1 tablespoon (15 ml) red wine
    vinegar
1 tablespoon (15 ml) extra-virgin
    olive oil
Salt and black pepper, to taste
3 tablespoons (23 g) pistachios,
    coarsely chopped
3 tablespoons (28 g) dried
    cranberries

1 Wash the quinoa in a large bowl, changing the water 3 times.

2 Add the quinoa and broth to a medium saucepan, and heat until boiling. Cover and cook over medium heat for 10 to 12 minutes, until the liquid is absorbed.

3 Meanwhile, in a separate pot, blanch the green beans for 2 minutes and cut into ½-inch (13 mm) pieces.

4 In a small bowl, whisk together the vinegar, oil, salt, and pepper.

5 Combine the cooked quinoa, green beans, pistachios, and cranberries, along with the vinaigrette.

PLAN AHEAD

1 Enjoy the Quinoa Salad and rotisserie chicken for dinner, and have leftovers for tomorrow's bento. The Quinoa Salad is good for a couple days, so make a larger batch if you like.
2 In the morning, make the green salad with tomatoes and feta cheese.

LOW-CARB BENTO

GRILLED SHRIMP AND STEAMED VEGETABLES BENTO

Grilled shrimp is an easy-to-make, tasty entrée for lunch or dinner. Adding a little butter at the end of cooking will give it a richer flavor. Instead of sautéing or stir-frying, steam the vegetables for a fresher taste and to enjoy their crispness. The miso and Parmesan dip has a great savory flavor and is a good accompaniment for the vegetables.

TO MAKE THIS BENTO

Each bento has a main-dish recipe (below), side-dish recipes (page 163), and additional ingredients.

Grilled Shrimp and Steamed Vegetables
  (see recipe below)
Miso and Parmesan Dip (see recipe below)

Apple slices and peanut butter
Parsley

PREP TIME: 10 MINUTES   **COOK TIME:** 13 MINUTES   **YIELD:** 2 SERVINGS

GRILLED SHRIMP AND STEAMED VEGETABLES WITH MISO AND PARMESAN DIP

MISO AND PARMESAN DIP

1 teaspoon miso
2 teaspoons grated
  Parmesan cheese
½ clove garlic, grated
2 tablespoons (28 g)
  mayonnaise
2 tablespoons (30 g) plain yogurt
1 teaspoon freshly
  squeezed lemon juice

GRILLED SHRIMP AND
STEAMED VEGETABLES

1 cup (90 g) chopped cabbage
4 spears asparagus, cut in half

½ cup (35 g) broccoli florets
½ cup (35 g) cauliflower
  florets
6 slices zucchini, ½ inch
  (13 mm) thick
6 slices yellow summer
  squash, ½ inch (13 mm)
  thick
6 to 8 large shrimp, peeled
  and deveined
Salt and black pepper, to taste
1 teaspoon vegetable oil
1 teaspoon sake (or cooking
  wine)
1 teaspoon butter

1. **To make the miso and Parmesan dip:** Mix together all the dip ingredients. Set aside.

2. **To make the shrimp and steamed vegetables:** Bring water to a boil in a large saucepan. Put all the vegetables in a vegetable basket for steaming and set aside. Lightly sprinkle the shrimp with salt and pepper and set aside.

3. Put the vegetable basket in the saucepan, over the boiling water. Cover and cook for 3 minutes. Remove the basket from the saucepan.

4. Heat the oil in a medium skillet over medium heat. Add the shrimp and cook for 2 to 3 minutes per side. Add the sake and butter, and stir for 30 seconds.

5. Serve the shrimp and steamed vegetables with the miso and Parmesan dip.

PLAN AHEAD

1. Make the Miso and Parmesan Dip and cut up the vegetables the night before.
2. In the morning, steam the vegetables, cook the shrimp, and slice the apple.

CAULIFLOWER FRIED RICE BENTO

Cauliflower fried rice is just like fried rice, except the rice is replaced with cauliflower crumbles. This is a great dish if you're limiting your carbohydrate intake.

TO MAKE THIS BENTO

Each bento has a main-dish recipe (below), side-dish recipes (page 163), and additional ingredients.

Cauliflower Fried Rice (see recipe below)	**4 lettuce leaves**
Braised Baby Bok Choy (page 170)	**Mixed berries**

PREP TIME: 7 MINUTES   **COOK TIME:** 8 MINUTES   **YIELD:** 2 SERVINGS

CAULIFLOWER FRIED RICE

½ large head cauliflower (or 1 bag, 8 ounces, or 227 g, cauliflower crumbles)
1 tablespoon (15 ml) vegetable oil
1 clove garlic, minced
5 ounces (150 g) ground pork
½ cup (75 g) frozen mixed vegetables
2 large eggs, beaten
¼ teaspoon salt
Pinch white pepper
2 teaspoons soy sauce
2 green onions, thinly sliced
Benishoga (pickled red ginger), for garnish

1 Chop the cauliflower into very small pieces, enough for 2 cups (170 g).

2 Heat the oil and garlic in a large skillet over medium heat. Add the ground pork and cook until browned.

3 Add the cauliflower and stir-fry for a couple minutes, until tender. Add the mixed vegetables and cook for 1 minute, then add the beaten eggs. Keep stir-frying until the eggs are cooked. Season with the salt, pepper, and soy sauce. Finally add the green onions and stir for a few seconds.

4 Top with the benishoga.

PLAN AHEAD

1 Enjoy Cauliflower Fried Rice for dinner, and have leftovers in tomorrow's bento. If you are going to make it in the morning, chop the vegetables the night before or use the cauliflower crumbles in a bag. You also can make the Braised Baby Bok Choy the night before.

2 In the morning, make or reheat the Cauliflower Fried Rice and reheat the Braised Baby Bok Choy.

FISH MEUNIÈRE BENTO

Meunière is a cooking technique used for fish dishes. Fillets of fish (often flat white fish) are dredged in flour (or cornstarch in this recipe) and fried in melted butter. The flat fish cooks quickly, so you can make it in the morning.

TO MAKE THIS BENTO

Each bento has a main-dish recipe (below), side-dish recipes (page 163), and additional ingredients.

Fish Meunière (see recipe below)
Sautéed Mushrooms and Asparagus (page 190)
Green salad with bean sprouts and tomato

Dressing of your choice
1 grapefruit, peeled

PREP TIME: 3 MINUTES   **COOK TIME:** 7 MINUTES   **YIELD:** 2 SERVINGS

FISH MEUNIÈRE

2 fillets (3.5 to 5 ounces, or
    100 to 150 g) red snapper or
    sole (or other thin white fish)
Salt and black pepper, to taste
2 tablespoons (30 ml) cornstarch
2 teaspoons vegetable oil
2 teaspoons butter
1 teaspoon chopped parsley,
    for garnish
2 slices lemon, for garnish

1 Cut each fillet into 2 pieces and pat dry with paper towels. Sprinkle both sides of the fish with salt and pepper. Lightly dredge the fish in cornstarch.

2 Heat the oil in a large skillet over medium heat. Add the fish and cook for about 3 minutes on one side. Flip, cover the pan, and cook for another 2 to 3 minutes.

3 Turn off the heat, add the butter, and coat the fish with the sauce. Garnish with the chopped parsley and lemon.

PLAN AHEAD

1 Because you can quickly make the Fish Meunière and Sautéed Mushrooms and Asparagus, everything can be made in the morning. To make it faster, cut the vegetables for the Sautéed Mushrooms and Asparagus and green salad the night before. The grapefruit also can be prepped in advance.

2 In the morning, cook the Fish Meunière and Sautéed Mushrooms and Asparagus.

LETTUCE WRAP BENTO

A Chinese-style lettuce wrap is usually made with cooked ground meat and vegetables in a cup-shaped lettuce leaf; here, the filling is wrapped completely with lettuce, like a burrito, so that it is easier to pack (and to eat) in a bento box. If you're having rice or bread (or another starch) with it, cut the serving in half.

TO MAKE THIS BENTO

Each bento has a main-dish recipe (below), side-dish recipes (page 163), and additional ingredients.

Lettuce Wrap (see recipe below)
Pickled Bell Pepper (page 201)
1 cup (155 g) cooked Edamame (page 172)

1 hard-boiled egg, sprinkled with black sesame seeds and salt

PREP TIME: 10 MINUTES   **COOK TIME:** 15 MINUTES   **YIELD:** 2 SERVINGS

LETTUCE WRAP

1 tablespoon (15 ml) sesame oil
¼ teaspoon minced garlic
¼ teaspoon minced ginger
14 ounces (400 g) ground chicken
6 shiitake mushrooms, finely chopped
4 ounces (117 g) takenoko (bamboo shoots), finely chopped
1 tablespoon (15 ml) soy sauce
2 tablespoons (30 ml) sake
2 tablespoons (36 g) oyster sauce
2 teaspoons sugar
6 green onions, finely chopped
8 lettuce leaves

1 Heat the oil, garlic, and ginger together in a large skillet over medium heat until the garlic and ginger start to color, about 30 seconds.

2 Add the chicken and cook for a couple minutes. Add the mushrooms and takenoko, and cook for an additional minute.

3 Add the soy sauce, sake, oyster sauce, and sugar, and stir-fry for a few minutes, then stir in the green onions. Remove from the heat.

4 Wrap one-quarter of the meat filling with 2 lettuce leaves like a burrito. Wrap tightly in plastic wrap, then cut in half. Repeat this step 3 more times with the remaining meat and lettuce leaves.

PLAN AHEAD

1 Make multiple batches of the Lettuce Wrap filling to enjoy for dinner and the next day's lunch.
2 Make the Pickled Bell Pepper, Edamame, and hard-boiled egg the night before.
3 In the morning, assemble the Lettuce Wraps.

CURRY CHICKEN SALAD BENTO

Curry chicken salad has become an American deli classic. With protein (chicken pieces), vitamins (grapes), and a nice curry aroma, this is the perfect lunch entrée to get you through the day. We recommend using store-bought rotisserie chicken for extra convenience.

TO MAKE THIS BENTO

Each bento has a main-dish recipe (below), side-dish recipes (page 163), and additional ingredients.

Curry Chicken Salad (see recipe below)
Cucumber and yellow bell pepper slices
Cornichons

Butter lettuce
Raspberries

PREP TIME: 10 MINUTES   **YIELD:** 2 SERVINGS

CURRY CHICKEN SALAD

2 tablespoons (28 g)
   mayonnaise
2 tablespoons (30 g) plain
   yogurt
1 teaspoon curry powder
1 teaspoon freshly squeezed
   lemon juice
¼ teaspoon salt
1½ cups (165 g) cubed rotisserie
   chicken
1 cup (150 g) green grapes,
   cut in half
10 to 15 toasted almonds,
   coarsely chopped

1 In a medium bowl, combine the mayonnaise, yogurt, curry powder, lemon juice, and salt. Add the diced chicken and grapes, and mix well.

2 Sprinkle the chopped almonds over the salad right before eating.

PLAN AHEAD

1 Enjoy rotisserie chicken for dinner, then cut up the leftovers after dinner for this salad. You can also slice the veggies the night before.

2 In the morning, mix up the Chicken Curry Salad. Don't mix in the almonds ahead of time because they will lose their crunchy texture.

BEEF AND VEGETABLE STIR-FRY BENTO

Beef and vegetable stir-fry is a popular home-cooking dish in Japan for its simplicity and healthiness. Even with the oil and beef, it is considered healthy because of the amount and variety of vegetables. Try to use fresh vegetables if you have time and add the fresh fruit to the bento for even more nutrition.

TO MAKE THIS BENTO

Each bento has a main-dish recipe (below), side-dish recipes (page 163), and additional ingredients.

Beef and Vegetable Stir-Fry (see recipe below)
2 large lettuce leaves

8 to 10 strawberries
6 to 8 orange segments

PREP TIME: 5 MINUTES   **COOK TIME:** 7 MINUTES   **YIELD:** 2 TO 4 SERVINGS

BEEF AND VEGETABLE STIR-FRY

10 ounces (300 g) beef (cut of choice), thinly sliced
2 teaspoons vegetable oil
¼ medium red bell pepper, cut into ½-inch-wide (13 mm) strips
¼ medium green bell pepper, cut into ½-inch-wide (13 mm) strips
⅓ medium carrot, thinly sliced
½ medium onion, thinly sliced
2 cups (180 g) chopped cabbage
¼ teaspoon salt
White pepper, to taste
1 teaspoon soy sauce

1 Cut the sliced beef into 3-inch-wide (7.5 cm) pieces.

2 Heat the oil in a wok or large skillet over medium heat. Add the beef and cook until browned.

3 Add the vegetables and stir-fry for 2 to 3 minutes. Season with the salt, pepper, and soy sauce. Cook for 30 seconds longer. Remove from the heat.

PLAN AHEAD

1 Leftover stir-fry may get wilted a bit, so try making it fresh in the morning. Prep the night before by cutting the veggies and meat, and then refrigerate them overnight. Now the dish will be done in less than 10 minutes in the morning. Prep the fruit in advance too.
2 In the morning, cook the Beef and Vegetable Stir-Fry.

VEGAN BENTO

TOFU STEAK SALAD BENTO

In this recipe, tofu is simply fried in some olive oil and seasoned with salt and pepper. Kale and crunchy vegetables tossed in a tangy, sweet vinaigrette, along with marinated mushrooms, add texture and umami to the dish.

TO MAKE THIS BENTO

Each bento has a main-dish recipe (below), side-dish recipes (page 163), and additional ingredients.

Tofu Steak Salad (see recipe below)
Onigiri (page 165), with black sesame seeds

Marinated Mushrooms (page 193)

PREP TIME: 10 MINUTES   **COOK TIME:** 6 MINUTES   **YIELD:** 2 SERVINGS

TOFU STEAK SALAD

14 ounces (396 g) firm tofu

2 tablespoons (30 ml) extra-virgin olive oil, divided

¼ teaspoon plus ⅛ teaspoon salt, divided

Black pepper, to taste

1 tablespoon (15 ml) freshly squeezed lemon juice

1 tablespoon (15 ml) apple cider vinegar

1 teaspoon honey

2 cups (80 g) chopped kale

1 cup (70 g) shredded red cabbage

¼ medium carrot, peeled and cut into matchsticks

1 Drain the tofu and cut it into 1-inch-thick (2.5 cm) thick rectangles. Pat dry with paper towels to remove excess moisture. Coat the surface with 1 tablespoon (15 ml) of the olive oil and sprinkle with ¼ teaspoon of the salt and the pepper.

2 Heat a grill pan or large skillet over medium heat. Add the tofu and cook for 2 to 3 minutes per side, until lightly browned. Remove from the heat and set aside.

3 In a bowl, mix together the lemon juice, vinegar, remaining 1 tablespoon (15 ml) olive oil, honey, remaining ⅛ teaspoon salt, and pepper to taste. Add the kale, red cabbage, and carrot, and combine. Place the salad and cooled tofu steak in the bento box.

PLAN AHEAD

1 The Marinated Mushrooms can be stored in the refrigerator for up to 4 to 5 days, so make a batch ahead of time. Make the Tofu Steak the day before and store in the refrigerator.
2 Before you go to bed, set the timer on the rice cooker for the Onigiri rice.
3 In the morning, prepare the Onigiri and toss the salad, placing the cold tofu on top.

FALAFEL BENTO

Falafel is a popular Middle Eastern dish made with ground chickpeas. It can be eaten by itself or with a salad, or you can stuff it in pita bread with some homemade hummus. Pack these bento components in separate compartments in a bento box and assemble while you eat.

TO MAKE THIS BENTO

Each bento has a main-dish recipe (below), side-dish recipes (page 163), and additional ingredients.

Falafel (see recipe below)	**Lettuce**
Hummus (page 203)	**Cherry tomatoes**
Pita bread	**Grapefruit segments**

PREP TIME: 20 MINUTES (PLUS SOAKING TIME)   **COOK TIME:** 10 MINUTES   **YIELD:** 2 SERVINGS

FALAFEL

1 cup (200 g) dried chickpeas
1 clove garlic, minced
1 jalapeño pepper, minced
   (optional)
¼ medium onion, chopped
¼ cup (15 g) chopped parsley
   and/or cilantro
½ teaspoon ground coriander
½ teaspoon ground cumin
½ teaspoon salt
2 tablespoons (30 ml)
   all-purpose flour
½ teaspoon baking powder
Vegetable oil, for frying

1. In a large bowl, combine the chickpeas with water to cover by at least 2 inches (5 cm). Soak overnight or up to 24 hours.

2. Place the drained chickpeas, garlic, jalapeño, onion, parsley and/or cilantro, coriander, cumin, and salt in a food processor. Pulse until minced and blended but not pureed.

3. Sprinkle the chickpea mixture with the flour and baking soda and pulse again until it forms a ball. Scoop the dough into heaping tablespoons and roll into balls.

4. Heat 1 to 2 inches (2.5 to 5 cm) of oil in a large skillet over medium-high heat and fry the falafel for 5 minutes, or until browned.

PLAN AHEAD

1. The Hummus can be made in advance and stored for up to 3 to 4 days in the refrigerator.
2. Enjoy Falafel for dinner, and have leftovers in tomorrow's bento. Alternatively, keep premade Falafel frozen in a freezer bag for up to a month and reheat in the oven.
3. In the morning, reheat the Falafel.

VEGETABLE MISO SOUP BENTO

Miso soup is a very important part of Japanese cuisine; it comes with almost every meal in Japan. Although you can use meat or fish in the soup, it is vegetarian-friendly because it is easy to skip the meat without missing much of its flavor. Make sure to use Kombu Dashi (page 21) for vegetarians and vegans, instead of Katsuo Dashi (bonito broth; page 20).

TO MAKE THIS BENTO

Each bento has a main-dish recipe (below), side-dish recipes (page 163), and additional ingredients.

Vegetable Miso Soup (see recipe below)
Onigiri (page 165), with salt and roasted seaweed

Fruit salad (grapefruit, kiwi, and blackberries)

PREP TIME: 10 MINUTES   **COOK TIME:** 10 MINUTES   **YIELD:** 2 SERVINGS

VEGETABLE MISO SOUP

2 cups (475 ml) Kombu Dashi (page 21)

½ bunch shimeji mushrooms, bottom removed and mushrooms separated into small pieces

1 cup (85 g) sliced kabocha squash (¼ × 2-inch, or 6 mm × 5 cm, pieces)

½ cup (65 g) quartered and sliced carrot (⅛-inch-thick, or 3 mm, pieces)

½ cup (50 g) quartered and sliced daikon radish (⅛-inch-thick, or 3 mm, pieces)

1 square aburaage (deep-fried tofu), thinly sliced

2 tablespoons (32 g) miso paste

1 green onion, finely chopped

1   Bring the kombu dashi broth to a boil in a medium saucepan over medium heat.

2   Add the mushrooms, squash, carrot, daikon and aburaage to the hot broth. Cook over medium heat for 3 to 4 minutes, until the vegetables are soft.

3   Reduce to heat to low and dissolve the miso paste in the soup. Take care not to let the soup boil.

4   Add the chopped green onion and remove the soup from the heat.

PLAN AHEAD

1   Enjoy Vegetable Miso Soup for dinner, along with extra broth and cut vegetables for tomorrow's bento, and keep in the refrigerator. (You can use day-old Miso Soup if you like, but it will taste fresher if you make it in the morning.)

2   Before you go to bed, set the timer on the rice cooker for the Onigiri rice.

3   In the morning, make or reheat the soup and use a soup jar to pack it, so it doesn't leak or get cold. In the meantime, make the Onigiri.

SPAGHETTI WITH LIMA BEANS AND CABBAGE BENTO

Lima beans are a great source of fiber and protein, and also a flexible ingredient for many dishes because of their mild flavor. This pasta dish is full of flavor from the garlic and red chile.

TO MAKE THIS BENTO

Each bento has a main-dish recipe (below), side-dish recipes (page 163), and additional ingredients.

Spaghetti with Lima Beans and Cabbage
   (see recipe below)
Carrot Kinpira (page 166)

6 to 8 blanched broccoli florets
6 to 8 grape tomatoes
2 lettuce leaves

PREP TIME: 10 MINUTES   **COOK TIME:** 15 MINUTES   **YIELD:** 2 SERVINGS

SPAGHETTI WITH LIMA BEANS AND CABBAGE

5 ounces (150 g) dried spaghetti
1 tablespoon (15 ml)
   extra-virgin olive oil
1 clove garlic, sliced
½ takanotsume (dried red chile
   pod), seeded and sliced
1 cup (90 g) chopped cabbage
½ cup (120 g) canned large lima
   beans (butter beans), drained
Salt, to taste

1 Bring a large saucepan of salted water to a boil (use 1 tablespoon, or 30 ml, salt per 1 quart, or 1 L, of water). Cook the spaghetti according to the package directions. Drain, reserving ¼ cup (60 ml) cooking water.

2 Three to 4 minutes before the pasta is done, heat the oil, garlic, and takanotsume in a large skillet over low heat. When the garlic just starts to brown, add the cabbage, raise the heat to medium, and cook for 1 minute. Add the lima beans and reserved pasta water, and cook for another minute. Add the cooked, drained spaghetti, stir, and season with salt as needed.

PLAN AHEAD

1 Enjoy a pasta dinner and save some plain cooked spaghetti for tomorrow's bento. Alternatively, boil pasta in the morning. Blanch the broccoli in the same water the pasta has cooked. Make the Carrot Kinpira the night before.
2 In the morning, cook the spaghetti dish.

HIJIKI GOHAN BENTO

Hijiki is a kind of seaweed that is full of nutrients, such as fiber, calcium, vitamins, and minerals. It's been eaten in Japan since ancient times, and it's one of the most commonly served side dishes in Japanese homes. Hijiki is typically simmered and strongly seasoned, so it makes a good accompaniment to steamed rice. Here, we mix simmered hijiki with rice (*gohan*), but you can also add simmered hijiki by itself as a side dish in bento.

TO MAKE THIS BENTO

Each bento has a main-dish recipe (below), side-dish recipes (page 163), and additional ingredients.

Hijiki Gohan (see recipe below)
Pan-Fried Kabocha (page 176)

Broccoli Namul (page 168)
Fresh fruits

PREP TIME: 20 MINUTES   **COOK TIME:** 15 MINUTES   **YIELD:** 2 SERVINGS

HIJIKI GOHAN

1 to 2 dried shiitake mushrooms
2 tablespoons (14 g) dried hijiki
    seaweed
1 teaspoon vegetable oil
⅓ medium carrot, julienned
1 tablespoon (15 ml) soy sauce
1 tablespoon (15 ml) mirin
1 tablespoon (15 ml) sake
1 teaspoon sugar
2 cups (330 g) Steamed Rice
    (page 18)
¼ cup (30 g) frozen shelled
    edamame, thawed

1 Rehydrate the dried shiitake mushrooms and hijiki in water, in separate bowls, for 15 minutes or longer. Strain, saving 2 tablespoons (30 ml) of the water used to rehydrate the shiitake mushrooms for cooking. (It's full of umami.) Thinly slice the shiitake mushrooms.

2 Heat the oil in a small skillet over medium heat. Add the hijiki, carrot, and shiitake, and cook and stir for 5 minutes. Add the reserved soaking water, soy sauce, mirin, sake, and sugar, and continue cooking over medium heat until the liquid is almost evaporated.

3 In a medium bowl, combine the rice, edamame, and hijiki.

PLAN AHEAD

1 Make the simmered hijiki in advance and keep in the refrigerator for a few days.
2 Make the Pan-Fried Kabocha and Broccoli Namul the day before.
3 Before you go to bed, set the timer on the rice cooker.
4 In the morning, combine the hijiki and rice.

TOFU POKE BENTO

Poke is a popular Hawaiian salad that has recently gained popularity elsewhere. Typical poke is made with raw fish, such as ahi tuna, but variations are endless. This tofu poke is vegan, and the best part is that you can pack it in a bento because there is no raw fish! Place the poke and toppings on steamed rice, and you will have a healthy and delicious poke bowl. Any vegetable toppings will do, but vinegary *sunomono* and fresh avocado always go well to balance the saltiness of the soy sauce in the poke.

TO MAKE THIS BENTO

Each bento has a main-dish recipe (below), side-dish recipes (page 163), and additional ingredients.

Tofu Poke (see recipe below)
Steamed Rice (page 18)
Cucumber and Radish Sunomono (page 199)

1 avocado, sliced
1 carrot, shredded

PREP TIME: 10 MINUTES   **YIELD:** 2 SERVINGS

TOFU POKE

---

8 ounces (227 g) firm or
   extra-firm tofu
1 tablespoon (15 ml) soy sauce
1½ teaspoons sesame oil
½ teaspoon red chile sauce,
   such as sriracha (optional)
½ teaspoon sesame seeds
Pinch salt
Pinch sugar
1 green onion, chopped
½ teaspoon grated fresh ginger

1 Drain, pat dry, and cut the tofu into ½-inch (13 mm) cubes.

2 In a medium bowl, combine the remaining ingredients.

3 Add the tofu and mix.

PLAN AHEAD

1 Make the Tofu Poke and Cucumber and Radish Sunomono the night before. You can also shred the carrot.
2 Before you go to bed, set the timer on the rice cooker.
3 In the morning, slice the avocado and assemble the Tofu Poke bowl.

BENTO FOR SPECIAL OCCASIONS

VALENTINE'S DAY BENTO

Surprise your loved ones with this decorative and tasty heart-shaped meatloaf on Valentine's Day! If you have a heart-shaped cookie cutter, this individually sized meatloaf is easy to make. Because it is smaller than a regular meatloaf, the time required for baking is shorter too. This meatloaf can be made ahead of time; it freezes well. Wrap cooked or uncooked meatloaf in plastic wrap and keep in the freezer for up 2 to 3 weeks.

TO MAKE THIS BENTO

Each bento has a main-dish recipe (below), side-dish recipes (page 163), and additional ingredients.

Heart-Shaped Meatloaf (see recipe below)	**Berries**
Macaroni Salad (page 180)	**Blanched broccoli**
	Dinner roll or small croissant

PREP TIME: 10 MINUTES   **COOK TIME:** 35 MINUTES   **YIELD:** TWO 3-INCH (7.5 CM) HEARTS

HEART-SHAPED MEATLOAF

½ teaspoon vegetable oil
¼ medium onion, finely chopped
¼ medium carrot, finely chopped
2 tablespoons (6 g) panko
1 tablespoon (15 ml) milk
5 ounces (150 g) ground beef
½ large egg
¼ teaspoon salt
Pinch pepper
2 tablespoons (30 ml) ketchup
2 slices cheese of choice

1 Preheat the oven to 350°F (180°C).

2 Heat the oil in a medium skillet over medium heat. Add the onion and carrot, and cook and stir until soft, about 3 minutes.

3 In a medium bowl, combine the panko with the milk and let sit for 3 minutes. Add the ground beef, onion-carrot mixture, egg, salt, and pepper. Mix well by hand.

4 Place a heart-shaped cookie cutter (3-inch, or 7.5 cm, diameter) on a baking sheet and stuff with the meat mixture. Press down using fingertips and remove the mold. Spread the ketchup on the surface of each meatloaf, transfer the baking sheet to the oven, and bake for 30 minutes. Cut the cheese into a heart shape smaller than the meatloaf and place on top.

PLAN AHEAD

1 Make the Macaroni Salad and blanch the broccoli the night before.
2 In the morning, cook or reheat the Meatloaf.

HALLOWEEN BENTO

You may not have time to make an elaborate *kyaraben* (character bento) every day, but on Halloween, spend a little extra time making a cute or scary onigiri to surprise your loved ones. *Gyoza* are Japanese dumplings that are typically filled with ground pork and chopped vegetables. This simple variation is vegetarian and made with kabocha and cheese, with a hint of curry.

TO MAKE THIS BENTO

Each bento has a main-dish recipe (below), side-dish recipes (page 163), and additional ingredients.

Black Cat Onigiri (see recipe below)
Kabocha and Cheese Gyoza (see recipe below)
Tako Sausage (page 196)

Cucumber slices and grape tomatoes, skewered
1 large lettuce leaf

PREP TIME: 20 MINUTES   **COOK TIME:** 10 MINUTES   **YIELD:** 2 SERVINGS

BLACK CAT ONIGIRI AND KABOCHA AND CHEESE GYOZA

KABOCHA AND CHEESE GYOZA
1 cup (85 g) peeled and cubed
  kabocha squash (1-inch, or
  2.5-cm, cubes)
½ cup (58 g) shredded cheese
  of choice
¼ cup (15 g) finely cut chives
½ teaspoon salt
½ teaspoon curry powder
6 to 8 gyoza wrappers
Vegetable oil, for frying

BLACK CAT ONIGIRI
2 pinches salt (1 per onigiri)
2 cups (330 g) warm Steamed
  Rice (page 18)
2 sheets nori (roasted seaweed)
1 slice cheese of choice

1 **To make the kabocha and cheese gyoza:** Place the kabocha in a microwave-safe bowl, cover, and microwave for 3 minutes. Mash with a fork and let cool. Stir in the shredded cheese, chives, salt, and curry powder.

2 Take a heaping teaspoon of the kabocha mixture and place in the middle of a gyoza wrapper. Moisten the edge of the wrapper with water, fold in half, and seal tightly. Repeat with the remaining kabocha mixture and wrappers.

3 Heat 2 inches (5 cm) of oil in a large skillet over medium heat. Fry the gyoza for 3 minutes, or until lightly browned.

4 **To make the black cat onigiri:** Wet your hands with water and sprinkle with a pinch of salt. Place half of the warm rice in one hand, press with both hands, and form into a 3-inch-wide (7.5 cm) oval shape. Press the top side using your fingers to shape 2 ears. Let cool. Repeat to make the second onigiri.

5 Place each onigiri on a sheet of nori and cut the nori sheets 1½ inches (3.5 cm) larger than the shape of the rice ball. Cut a few slits around the corners and press the nori on the rice. Squeeze lightly to shape. Place the onigiri, nori side up, in the bento box.

6 Cut the cheese and remaining nori to make eyes and place them on the onigiri.

PLAN AHEAD

1 The Kabocha and Cheese Gyoza can be prepared ahead of time and frozen. Place the uncooked gyoza on a baking sheet and freeze for 1 hour, or until they are hard. Store in a freezer bag for up to 1 month. Fry the frozen gyoza in the morning without defrosting.

2 Before you go to bed, make the Tako Sausage and set the timer on the rice cooker for the Onigiri rice.

3 In the morning, make the Onigiri Black Cats, fry the Kabocha and Cheese Gyoza, and reheat the Tako Sausage.

BIRTHDAY BENTO

Make a special sandwich lunch for someone's birthday! Here, a simple ham sandwich is transformed into a tiered birthday cake. There is a lot of cutting (even using cookie cutters), but it's easy to do.

TO MAKE THIS BENTO

Each bento has a main-dish recipe (below), side-dish recipes (page 163), and additional ingredients.

Sandwich Cake (see recipe below)
Popcorn Shrimp (page 188)
Mini Tomato Cups with Cottage Cheese (page 174)

Orange segments
1 large lettuce leaf

PREP TIME: 15 MINUTES   YIELD: 1 SERVING

SANDWICH CAKE

3 slices bread (preferably
  shokupan)
2 to 3 slices ham
1½ teaspoons mayonnaise
  (preferably Japanese)
2 slices provolone cheese
1 slice Cheddar cheese
5 very thin slices cucumber

1 From the bread, cut out two 3½-inch (9 cm) rounds and two 2-inch (5 cm) rounds with cookie cutters. Repeat this step with the ham slices. Spread the mayo on one side of each round of bread. Sandwich the large ham rounds between the large bread rounds, and the small ham rounds between the small bread rounds. Set aside.

2 Cut out 2 rounds of provolone cheese, one slightly smaller than the large bread rounds and another slightly smaller than the small bread rounds. Cut out a tiny round of Cheddar cheese. Cut out a round of ham in between the size of the small provolone round and the Cheddar round. Place the large provolone round on top of the large sandwich, and arrange the 5 cucumber slices like a flower on top of the provolone cheese. Place the small sandwich on top of the cucumber, then place the small provolone, ham, and Cheddar rounds on top of the small sandwich. Pin the whole stack with a stick.

PLAN AHEAD

1 Prep the Popcorn Shrimp through step 2 the night before.
2 In the morning, make the Sandwich Cake and Mini Tomato Cups with Cottage Cheese, and fry the Popcorn Shrimp.

PICNIC OR FIELD TRIP BENTO

Teriyaki wings are fried chicken wings coated in a teriyaki sauce. This savory, casual finger food is perfect for a picnic. Actually, everything in this bento can be eaten with the hands. Pack the lunch in a disposable container if you don't want to carry an empty bento box all day.

TO MAKE THIS BENTO

Each bento has a main-dish recipe (below), side-dish recipes (page 163), and additional ingredients.

Teriyaki Wings (see recipe below)
Onigiri (page 165), with choice of filling
Tamagoyaki (page 22)

Cucumber slices and grape tomatoes, skewered
Edamame (page 172), skewered
Seasonal fruits

PREP TIME: 10 MINUTES   **COOK TIME:** 8 MINUTES   **YIELD:** 2 SERVINGS

TERIYAKI WINGS

Salt
6 to 8 chicken wings
2 tablespoons (30 ml) soy sauce
2 tablespoons (30 ml) mirin
1 tablespoon (15 ml) sake
1 tablespoon (15 ml) sugar
½ teaspoon grated garlic
½ teaspoon grated fresh ginger
1 teaspoon sesame seeds
Vegetable oil, for frying

1 Sprinkle a couple pinches of salt over the chicken wings and massage the salt into the wings. Let sit for 5 minutes.

2 In a small saucepan, bring the soy sauce, mirin, sake, sugar, garlic, ginger, and sesame seeds to a boil, then boil for 1 minute. Remove from the heat and set aside.

3 Heat 1 inch (2.5 cm) of oil in a large skillet over medium heat. Add the wings and fry for 4 minutes, turning a couple times. Increase the heat to high, and cook for another 2 minutes, or until cooked through.

4 Coat the freshly fried wings in the sauce.

PLAN AHEAD

1 The sauce, skewered vegetables, and fruit can be prepped the night before.
2 Before you go to bed, set the timer on the rice cooker for the Onigiri rice.
3 In the morning, fry the Teriyaki Wings and make the Onigiri and Tamagoyaki.

FIRST DAY OF SCHOOL BENTO

Here are some tips on what to pack in a bento filled with love for little children who are starting school, especially for the first time:

- Pack something they like.
- Don't overpack. You don't want to make them feel bad for not finishing the food you made.
- Make it fun (just a little). It takes only a few extra minutes to cut out sandwiches into fun shapes or mold hard-boiled eggs.

These homemade fruit snacks are healthier than store-bought versions and are naturally sweetened! Silicone candy molds are available in many different shapes.

TO MAKE THIS BENTO

Each bento has a main-dish recipe (below), side-dish recipes (page 163), and additional ingredients.

Fruit Snacks (see recipe below)
Cut-out sandwiches (nut-butter and jelly
  sandwiches, cut with cookie cutters)

Hard-boiled egg, shaped in a mold
Cheese of choice, cubed
Vegetable of choice, cut into sticks

PREP TIME: 10 MINUTES (PLUS 1 HOUR OR UP TO OVERNIGHT COOLING)　　**COOK TIME:** 5 MINUTES
YIELD: 2 SERVINGS

FRUIT SNACKS

½ cup (120 ml) juice of choice
1 tablespoon (6 g) gelatin
1 tablespoon (20 g) honey

1 In a small saucepan, add the juice and sprinkle with the gelatin. Let the gelatin bloom for 3 minutes.

2 Heat over low heat, stirring constantly, until the gelatin melts. (Do not boil.)

3 Transfer the liquid to silicone candy molds. Refrigerate for 1 hour or overnight and remove from the molds.

PLAN AHEAD

1 Make a large batch of fruit snacks ahead of time and keep them in the refrigerator.
2 Hard-boil the egg, cut the vegetable sticks, and cube the cheese the night before.
3 In the morning, make the cut-out sandwiches.

BENTO AT HOME

TEMPURA BENTO

Tempura is a popular Japanese food in and outside of Japan, and the perfect dish for entertaining guests. Lightly battered and fried seafood and vegetables are delicious when done right and fresh.

TO MAKE THIS BENTO

Each bento has a main-dish recipe (below), side-dish recipes (page 163), and additional ingredients.

Tempura (see recipe below)
Steamed Rice (page 18), with black sesame seeds

Vegetable Nimono (page 172)
Octopus and Cucumber Sunomono (page 185)

PREP TIME: 10 MINUTES   **COOK TIME:** 20 MINUTES   **YIELD:** 4 SERVINGS

TEMPURA

⅓ cup (80 ml) Mentsuyu (page 204)
⅔ cup (160 ml) water
12 large tail-on shrimp, deveined
8 shiitake mushrooms
1 satsumaimo (Japanese sweet potato), sliced into ¼-inch-thick (6 mm) rounds (at least 8 rounds)
16 green beans, ends trimmed
1½ cups (180 g) cake flour
2 teaspoons baking soda
½ teaspoon salt
1½ cups (350 ml) ice water
Vegetable oil, for frying

1 Mix together the mentsuyu and water. Set aside.

2 Make diagonal cuts on the shrimp to help straighten them. Make several cuts for star decorations on the caps of the shiitake mushrooms. Carefully dry the shrimp and vegetables to remove any moisture.

3 In a medium bowl, whisk together the cake flour, baking powder, and salt. Add the ice water to the flour mixture and stir with chopsticks (not a whisk) until the flour is just incorporated (lumps are okay), taking care not to overmix.

4 Heat 2 inches (5 cm) of oil in a large skillet over medium-high heat (375°F, or 190°C). Dip the vegetables and shrimp in batter, then fry until they float and are cooked through. Serve with the mentsuyu-water dipping sauce.

PLAN AHEAD

1 The Vegetable Nimono can be made earlier in the day or the night before. Just heat up before serving. Prepare the Sunomono earlier in the day and chill.

2 Fry the Tempura just before serving. Have Mentsuyu stocked in your refrigerator. In the meantime, make the Steamed Rice.

TEMARI SUSHI BENTO

Temari sushi (or *temarizushi*) are small, round-shaped sushi that resemble *temari* balls, traditional Japanese hand balls made with colorful and decorative fabric. You top them with anything you like, such as sliced sashimi, thinly sliced vegetables, or cooked seafood or meat. Think of different colors, textures, and flavor combination when choosing the toppings. Feel free to be totally creative and have fun with it! While beautifully decorated temari sushi may look fancy, you don't need to be a sushi chef to make these. They are easy to make at home. Place your creations in a large enough box to share and your guests will surely be impressed!

TO MAKE THIS BENTO

Each bento has a main-dish recipe (below), side-dish recipes (page 163), and additional ingredients.

Temari Sushi (see recipe below)

PREP TIME: 1 HOUR   **COOK TIME:** 30 MINUTES   **YIELD:** 4 SERVINGS

TEMARI SUSHI

TOPPING OPTIONS

Sashimi slices, such as salmon,
    tuna, and yellowtail
Kinshi Tamago (page 194)
Boiled shrimp, butterflied
    along the belly side
Boiled octopus, thinly sliced
Avocado, thinly sliced
Cucumber, thinly sliced
Shiso leaves
Lemon slices, for garnish
Nori (roasted seaweed),
    for garnish

Sushi Rice (page 164; double
    the ingredients)

1 Place a sheet of plastic wrap on a flat surface and place a topping of choice or a combination of toppings (e.g., shrimp and avocado) on the plastic.

2 Place a heaping tablespoon of sushi rice on the topping(s). Gather the edges of the plastic wrap and twist in the middle to shape into a ball. Unwrap and top with garnish where needed.

PLAN AHEAD

Prepare the toppings earlier in the day and keep them refrigerated until you are ready to assemble the Temari Sushi, right before serving.

ROAST BEEF BENTO

Roast beef is a popular American dish, but it is also seen on the Japanese dinner table, especially on special occasions. Here, the roast beef is extra sumptuous using the tenderloin cut. It is important to watch temperatures at each stage to achieve the perfect doneness for the beef. Cooking time may vary depending on the shape and size of meat, how you like your meat cooked, and even your oven, so check the meat temperature!

TO MAKE THIS BENTO

Each bento has a main-dish recipe (below), side-dish recipes (page 163), and additional ingredients.

Roast Beef with Wasabi Cream Sauce
  (see recipe below)
Onigiri (page 165)
Fried Potato Balls (page 164)

Spinach and Arugula Salad with Lotus Root
  Chips (page 179)
Miso Walnuts (page 204)

PREP TIME: 15 MINUTES (PLUS 1 TO 2 HOURS RESTING)   **COOK TIME:** 55 MINUTES   **YIELD:** 4 SERVINGS

ROAST BEEF WITH WASABI CREAM SAUCE

ROAST BEEF

About 2 pounds (907 g) beef
  tenderloin
Salt and black pepper, to taste
2 cloves garlic, grated
2 tablespoons (30 ml) vegetable oil

WASABI CREAM SAUCE

½ cup (115 g) sour cream
2 tablespoons (30 ml) heavy
  cream
½ teaspoon wasabi paste
¼ teaspoon salt
Chopped chives, for garnish

1 **To make the roast beef:** Tie the meat with cotton cooking twine to keep a nice log shape. Season the meat liberally with salt and pepper, and rub with the garlic. Allow the meat to come to room temperature, 1 to 2 hours before roasting. Preheat the oven to 275°F (140°C) at least 30 minutes before roasting.

2 Heat the oil in a large skillet until very hot. Add the meat and sear the surface on all sides to brown it, 8 to 10 minutes.

3 Place a meat rack on a baking sheet, and put the seared meat on the rack. Transfer the baking sheet to the oven and roast for 40 to 45 minutes, checking the temperature after 35 minutes. The internal temperature should reach 125 to 130°F (52 to 55°C).

4 Cover the meat with aluminum foil to keep it warm and let sit for 1 hour.

5 **To make the wasabi cream sauce:** Combine all the sauce ingredients except for the chopped chives. Set aside.

6 Slice the roast beef and serve with the wasabi cream sauce topped with the chives.

PLAN AHEAD

Just like when you are making a holiday feast, prepare the main dish and side dishes at the same time. You will have plenty of time to make the side dishes while preparing the Roast Beef, especially when bringing the meat to room temperature and roasting it. When frying the Fried Potato Balls, the lotus chips can be fried at the same time. Fried foods are always at their best when served hot, so make them just before serving. The Spinach and Arugula Salad should be mixed with the dressing at the last minute also; otherwise, the greens will wilt.

SASHIMI BENTO

Sashimi is a traditional Japanese dish of thinly sliced raw meat or seafood. Fish sashimi is a popular item served at Japanese restaurants. While it's not ideal to pack raw fish in a portable bento box for work or school (as it's difficult to keep its freshness), sashimi is a great main dish to serve at home. You need to purchase fish specifically marked as sushi- or sashimi-grade from a specialty seafood store or Japanese/Asian market for safety. Freshly prepared assorted sashimi along with a few small authentic Japanese side dishes and rice in a traditional lacquered bento box will surely impress your guests!

TO MAKE THIS BENTO

Each bento has a main-dish recipe (below), side-dish recipes (page 163), and additional ingredients.

Assorted Sashimi (see recipe below)
Simmered Koya Tofu and Shiitake Mushrooms
  (page 192)

Miso Baked Chicken (page 194)
Steamed Rice (page 18), with black sesame
  seeds

PREP TIME: 5 MINUTES   **COOK TIME:** 13 MINUTES   **YIELD:** 2 SERVINGS

ASSORTED SASHIMI

4-inch (10 cm) length daikon
  radish
1 pound (454 g) sashimi- or
  sushi-grade fish, such as
  salmon, tuna, and
  red snapper
8 to 12 shiso leaves
Soy sauce
Wasabi paste

1 Peel the daikon and cut as thinly as possible lengthwise, then cut the slices into very thin strips. Immediately soak the strips in a bowl of cold water for a few minutes to crisp. Drain.

2 Slice the fish against the grain, about ⅓ inch (8 mm) thick.

3 Lay the shredded daikon and some shiso leaves on a plate and top with the sliced fish. Serve with soy sauce and wasabi for dipping the fish.

PLAN AHEAD

Prepping for the side dishes can start the day before or in the morning the day of serving this bento for dinner. Rehydrating the shiitake mushrooms and marinating the chicken can be done overnight in the refrigerator. The Simmered Koya Tofu and Shiitake Mushrooms can also be made the day before.

HOLIDAY BENTO

For a casual lunch for a holiday, this rolled turkey works well. It is a much easier and lighter fare than a feast with a whole bird. And you will have plenty of vegetables from the side dishes. Serving this with an appetizer and dessert will make the meal even more satisfying and festive.

TO MAKE THIS BENTO

Each bento has a main-dish recipe (below), side-dish recipes (page 163), and additional ingredients.

Rolled Turkey (see recipe below)
Mashed Kabocha Squash (page 173)
Sautéed Asparagus with Lemon and Butter (page 171)

Green salad with tomatoes
Choice of dressing
Dinner rolls

PREP TIME: 25 MINUTES   **COOK TIME:** 40 TO 45 MINUTES (PLUS 20 MINUTES RESTING)   **YIELD:** 4 SERVINGS

ROLLED TURKEY

2 cups (100 g) cubed bread
   (½-inch, or 13 mm cubes)
2 turkey breast tenderloins
   (about 10 ounces, or 300 g,
   each)
1 tablespoon (15 ml) butter
½ large yellow onion, chopped
1 celery rib, chopped
⅓ cup (20 g) chopped fresh
   parsley
½ teaspoon chopped fresh
   thyme
⅓ cup (50 g) dried cranberries
1 large egg
¾ cup (175 ml) chicken broth
¼ to ½ teaspoon salt, plus
   more to taste
Extra-virgin olive oil
Black pepper, to taste

1 Preheat the oven to 375ºF (190ºC). Bake the bread cubes until dry and lightly toasted, 7 to 8 minutes.

2 Slice through the thickest part of turkey tenders, butterflying them. Cover the meat with plastic wrap and pound with a meat mallet to ½ inch (13 mm) thick. Set aside.

3 Heat a small skillet over medium heat and add the butter. When the butter melts, add the onion and celery, and cook until soft.

4 In a large bowl, combine the toasted bread cubes, onion-celery mixture, parsley, thyme, cranberries, egg, chicken broth, and ¼ to ½ teaspoon of the salt until combined well.

5 Lay the turkey flat, with a long side toward you, and spread the filling on the meat. (Leftover filling can be baked in its own dish.) From the near end, start rolling the turkey to the other end, as if you were rolling a jelly-roll, tucking the bottom under. Tie with cotton cooking twine to make a nice log shape. Repeat this step with the second turkey tenderloin.

6 Coat the meat with plenty of olive oil and sprinkle with salt and pepper. Place on a baking sheet, transfer to the oven, and bake for 40 to 45 minutes, or until the internal temperature reaches 160ºF (71ºC). Remove the meat from the oven, cover with aluminum foil, and let rest for 20 minutes. Remove the twine and slice.

PLAN AHEAD

Because the turkey breast doesn't take a long time to cook, the whole meal will be ready in 90 minutes, which is not bad for a holiday feast. There is not much to do ahead of time because you can make all the side dishes while the meat is in the oven. If you would like, you can prep by toasting the bread cubes and pumpkin seeds and steaming the pumpkin the day before.

SIDE DISHES

RICE AND POTATOES

SUSHI RICE

PREP TIME: 5 MINUTES   **COOK TIME:** 15 MINUTES   **YIELD:** 2 SERVINGS

3 tablespoons (45 ml) rice
  vinegar
1 tablespoon (15 ml) sugar
½ teaspoon salt
2 cups (330 g) Steamed Rice
  (page 18)

1 Whisk together the rice vinegar, sugar, and salt until the sugar dissolves.

2 Transfer the freshly cooked hot rice to a large bowl and add the vinegar mixture into the rice, mixing lightly without mashing the rice. Let cool for 10 minutes.

FRIED POTATO BALLS

PREP TIME: 20 MINUTES   **COOK TIME:** 15 MINUTES   **YIELD:** 4 SERVINGS

½ pound (227 g) white potatoes
1½ tablespoons (23 ml) potato
  starch
1 tablespoon (8 g) grated
  Parmesan cheese
¼ teaspoon salt
White pepper
Vegetable oil, for frying

1 Cut each of the potatoes into 6 pieces and boil until soft. Drain.

2 Peel the potatoes and mash well while hot. Add the potato starch, cheese, salt, and pepper, and mix well. Roll into tablespoon-size balls.

3 Heat 2 inches (5 cm) of oil in a large saucepan over medium heat (350°F, or 180°C). Using a slotted spoon, submerge the potato balls in the oil for few seconds so that they don't stick to the bottom of the pan. Cook until golden brown.

ONIGIRI

PREP TIME: 1 HOUR   **COOK TIME:** 5 MINUTES   **YIELD:** 2 SERVINGS

2 cups (330 g) Steamed Rice
  (page 18), white or brown
Salt
Choice of filling:
  Umeboshi (pickled sour plum),
  Kombu Tsukudani (page 188),
  Okaka (page 184), or Salmon
  Flakes (page 54)
4 sheets nori, about 2 × 4 inches
  (5 × 10 cm)

1 Place the rice in a bowl and set aside for a few minutes until it's cool enough to handle.

2 Wet your hands with water and sprinkle with salt. Place one-quarter of the cooled rice in one hand, and use both hands to press and form the rice into a triangle shape.

3 Make a well in the middle of the rice ball and put a filling in the well. Close the well. Reshape as needed and wrap with a sheet of nori. Repeat steps 2 and 3 to make 4 onigiri.

VEGETABLES

CARROT NAMUL

PREP TIME: 3 MINUTES   **COOK TIME:** 2 MINUTES   **YIELD:** 2 SERVINGS

1 medium carrot, cut into
   matchsticks
1 teaspoon soy sauce
1 teaspoon sesame oil
1 teaspoon vinegar

1 Blanch the carrot until tender, drain, and place in a small bowl.

2 Add the remaining ingredients and combine.

CARROT KINPIRA

PREP TIME: 3 MINUTES   **COOK TIME:** 5 MINUTES   **YIELD:** 2 SERVINGS

1 medium carrot
1 teaspoon vegetable oil
2 teaspoons soy sauce
2 teaspoons sake
2 teaspoons mirin
1 tablespoon (15 ml) water
1 teaspoon sesame seeds

1 Cut the carrot into ⅛-inch-thick (3 mm) matchsticks.

2 Heat the oil in a small skillet over medium-low heat. Add the carrot and cook for a few minutes. Add the soy sauce, sake, mirin, and water, and cook and stir until the liquid has evaporated.

3 Remove from the heat, sprinkle with the sesame seeds, and mix.

SAUTÉED GREEN BEANS WITH SESAME SEEDS

PREP TIME: 5 MINUTES   **COOK TIME:** 3 MINUTES   **YIELD:** 2 SERVINGS

1 teaspoon sesame oil
10 green beans, blanched
    and cut into 2-inch (5 cm)
    lengths
Salt, to taste
½ teaspoon sesame seeds,
    for garnish

1 Heat the oil in a small skillet over medium heat.

2 Cook and stir the green beans for a couple minutes, then season with salt and sprinkle with the sesame seeds.

BROCCOLI NAMUL

PREP TIME: 2 MINUTES   COOK TIME: 2 MINUTES   YIELD: 2 SERVINGS

1 cup (70 g) broccoli florets
2 teaspoons vinegar
1 teaspoon soy sauce
1 teaspoon sesame oil

1 Blanch the broccoli until tender, drain, and place in a small bowl.

2 Add the remaining ingredients and mix.

BUTTERED BROCCOLI

PREP TIME: 2 MINUTES   COOK TIME: 2 MINUTES   YIELD: 2 SERVINGS

1 cup (70 g) broccoli florets
1½ teaspoons butter
Salt and black pepper, to taste

1 Blanch the broccoli until tender, drain, and transfer to a small bowl.

2 Add the remaining ingredients and mix.

GREEN BEANS WITH SESAME SAUCE

PREP TIME: 7 MINUTES   **COOK TIME:** 3 MINUTES   **YIELD:** 2 SERVINGS

¼ pound (113 g) green beans
1½ teaspoons soy sauce
1 teaspoon sugar
1½ teaspoons ground sesame seeds
Sesame seeds, for garnish

1 Cook the green beans in boiling water for 2 to 3 minutes. Drain. Cut into 2-inch-long (5 cm) pieces.

2 In a medium bowl, mix together the soy sauce, sugar, and ground sesame seeds. Add the green beans and combine.

3 Sprinkle the sesame seeds on top.

DAIKON AND CARROT NIMONO

PREP TIME: 3 MINUTES   **COOK TIME:** 20 MINUTES   **YIELD:** 2 SERVINGS

½ cup (120 ml) Dashi (page 20)
1 teaspoon sugar
1 tablespoon (15 ml) soy sauce
1 tablespoon (15 ml) sake
1 tablespoon (15 ml) mirin
½ cup (50 g) chopped (into bite-size pieces) daikon
½ cup (65 g) chopped (into bite-size pieces) carrot

1 In a small saucepan, bring the dashi, sugar, soy sauce, sake, and mirin to a boil.

2 Add the daikon and carrot and simmer for 20 minutes. Drain.

BRAISED BABY BOK CHOY

PREP TIME: 2 MINUTES   **COOK TIME:** 4 MINUTES   **YIELD:** 2 SERVINGS

3 baby bok choy
½ teaspoon potato starch
   (or cornstarch)
2 tablespoons (30 ml) plus
   1 teaspoon water, divided
1 teaspoon vegetable oil
1 teaspoon soy sauce
1 teaspoon sake
½ teaspoon sesame oil

1 Trim the bottoms of the baby bok choy and separate the leaves. Cut the leaves in half to separate the leafy parts and stems. Cut the stems in half lengthwise.

2 Mix the potato starch and 1 teaspoon of the water in a small bowl to make a slurry. Set aside.

3 Heat the oil in a large skillet over medium heat. Add the baby bok choy and cook for 1 minute. Add the remaining 2 tablespoons (30 ml) water, soy sauce, and sake. When the bok choy softens, add the potato starch slurry and stir until thickened. Stir in the sesame oil. Remove from the heat.

MISO EGGPLANT AND SHISHITO PEPPERS

PREP TIME: 3 MINUTES   **COOK TIME:** 7 MINUTES   **YIELD:** 2 SERVINGS

8 shishito peppers
2 cups (300 g) chopped (cut
   into small wedges) eggplant
   (preferably Japanese)
1 tablespoon (15 ml) vegetable oil
2 tablespoons (30 ml) water
2 tablespoons (32 g) miso paste
3 tablespoons (45 ml) mirin

1 Cut off the pepper stems, then cut the peppers in half if bigger than 4 inches (10 cm) big.

2 Heat the oil in a medium skillet over medium heat. Add the eggplant and stir-fry for 1 minute. Add the water and cover for 2 minutes. Add the peppers and cook for a few additional minutes. Add the miso and mirin, and stir until well mixed.

SAUTÉED ASPARAGUS WITH LEMON AND BUTTER

PREP TIME: 7 MINUTES   **COOK TIME:** 3 MINUTES   **YIELD:** 4 SERVINGS

24 spears asparagus
1 tablespoon (15 g) butter
Salt and black pepper, to taste
2 teaspoons freshly squeezed
   lemon juice
Lemon zest, for garnish

1 Blanch the asparagus for 1 minute. Drain. Trim the woody part from the bottom of each spear, then cut each spear in half crosswise.

2 Melt the butter in a large skillet over medium heat. Add the asparagus and cook and stir for 1 minute. Season with salt and pepper to taste. Remove from the heat and add the lemon juice. Garnish with the lemon zest.

VEGETABLE NIMONO

PREP TIME: 10 MINUTES   **COOK TIME:** 35 MINUTES   **YIELD:** 4 SERVINGS

12 snow peas
Pinch salt
1 to 1½ large carrots
1 bamboo shoot, boiled
1 lotus root, at least 6 inches
   (15 cm) long
1½ cups (350 ml) Dashi
   (page XX)
1 tablespoon (15 ml) sugar
2 tablespoons (30 ml) soy sauce
1 tablespoon (15 ml) sake
2 tablespoons (30 ml) mirin

1 Blanch the snow peas with the pinch of salt. Set aside.

2 Cut the carrot into twelve ½-inch-thick (13 mm) rounds, then cut the rounds with a small flower-shaped cookie cutter. Cut off the top 3 inches (7.5 cm) of the bamboo shoot and vertically cut this piece into 8 pieces. Use the remaining bamboo shoot for another dish. Slice the lotus root into twelve ½-inch-thick (13 mm) rounds.

3 Heat the dashi in a medium saucepan over medium heat. Add the bamboo shoot and lotus root. Cover partially and cook for 10 minutes. Add the carrot and cook another 10 minutes.

4 Season with the sugar, soy sauce, sake, and mirin, and stir. Cook uncovered for another 10 to 15 minutes. Remove from the heat and let it cool, covered, so the vegetables absorb flavor from the soup. Serve garnished with the snow peas.

EDAMAME

COOK TIME: 5 MINUTES   **YIELD:** 2 SERVINGS

1 cup (120 g) frozen edamame
Salt, to taste

1 In a medium saucepan, bring lightly salted water to a boil.

2 Add the frozen edamame and cook for 5 minutes. Drain and sprinkle with salt to taste.

MASHED KABOCHA SQUASH

PREP TIME: 30 MINUTES   **COOK TIME:** 10 MINUTES   **YIELD:** 4 SERVINGS

1 kabocha squash (about
   2 pounds, or 907 g)
¼ teaspoon salt
1 teaspoon sugar
1 tablespoon (15 g) butter
1 tablespoon (15 ml) heavy cream
2 tablespoons (28 g) toasted
   pumpkin seeds, for garnish

1 Cut the kabocha into 2-inch (5 cm) cubes, and steam until soft. Let cool for 10 minutes. Scoop out the flesh and discard the skin.

2 Put the kabocha flesh in a large saucepan with the salt and sugar. Mash and cook over medium heat until the consistency is similar to mashed potatoes. Add the butter and cream, and cook for another couple minutes. Top with the pumpkin seeds.

KABOCHA NIMONO

PREP TIME: 5 MINUTES   **COOK TIME:** 25 MINUTES   **YIELD:** 2 SERVINGS

½ pound (227 g) kabocha squash
1 cup (235 ml) Dashi (page 20)
1½ teaspoons sugar
1½ teaspoons soy sauce
1 teaspoon sake
Pinch salt

1 Remove the seeds from the kabocha and cut into 1½-inch (4 cm) cubes. Cut off the hard edges and corners of the pieces, if you want them rounder and smooth.

2 In a medium saucepan, bring the dashi to a boil. Add the kabocha. Cover and cook over medium heat until the kabocha is tender, 10 to 15 minutes.

3 Add the sugar, soy sauce, sake, and salt. Reduce the heat to medium-low and cook, uncovered, for another 10 minutes. Remove from the heat, cover, and let cool completely.

MINI TOMATO CUPS WITH COTTAGE CHEESE

PREP TIME: 5 MINUTES   **YIELD:** 2 SERVINGS

3 to 4 tablespoons (42 to 56 g)
cottage cheese
4 cherry tomatoes
Fresh parsley, for garnish

1 Spread the cottage cheese on a paper towel to remove some moisture.

2 Slice off the tops of the tomatoes. Scoop out the insides with a paring knife.

3 Stuff the tomatoes with the cottage cheese. Top with parsley leaves.

SATSUMAIMO AMANI

PREP TIME: 2 MINUTES   **COOK TIME:** 3 MINUTES   **YIELD:** 2 SERVINGS

½ satsumaimo (Japanese
sweet potato)
1 cup (235 ml) water, plus
additional to boil satsumaimo
2 tablespoons (30 ml) sugar
½ teaspoon soy sauce
Pinch salt

1 Cut the satsumaimo into ½-inch-thick (13 mm) slices, then cut the slices into halves or quarters if needed. Immediately soak in water in a medium saucepan, then turn on the heat and bring to a boil. Let boil for 2 minutes and drain.

2 In a clean medium saucepan, mix together the 1 cup (235 ml) water, sugar, soy sauce, and salt, and bring to a boil. Add the satsumaimo and cook for 10 minutes. Remove from the heat and let cool in the syrup.

SPINACH OHITASHI

PREP TIME: 7 MINUTES   COOK TIME: 3 MINUTES   YIELD: 2 TO 4 SERVINGS

½ bunch (6 ounces, or 170 g)
   spinach
1 tablespoon (15 ml) Mentsuyu
   (page 204)
2 tablespoons (30 ml) water
Pinch sugar
Katsuobushi (dried bonito flakes),
   for garnish

1 Blanch the spinach in boiling water for 15 seconds. Drain and let cool under running water. Squeeze out the water well from the spinach. Trim the roots (if any) and cut the spinach into 2-inch (5 cm) sections.

2 Combine the mentsuyu, water, and sugar in a bowl, then add the spinach. Mix well.

3 Chill or serve right away with a sprinkle of katsuobushi.

MARINATED ASPARAGUS

PREP TIME: 2 MINUTES   **COOK TIME:** 2 MINUTES   **YIELD:** 2 SERVINGS

12 to 15 stalks asparagus,
   trimmed and cut into 2½-inch
   (6 cm) pieces
Pinch salt
Black pepper, to taste
2 teaspoons extra-virgin olive oil
1 teaspoon balsamic vinegar

Blanch the asparagus until tender, drain, and place in a small bowl. Add the remaining ingredients and mix.

PAN-FRIED KABOCHA

PREP TIME: 2 MINUTES   **COOK TIME:** 10 MINUTES   **YIELD:** 2 SERVINGS

1 teaspoon vegetable oil
⅛ kabocha squash, sliced ½ inch
   (13 mm) thick
Salt and black pepper, to taste

1 Heat the oil in a small skillet over medium heat. Add the kabocha and cook for 5 minutes per side.

2 Season with salt and pepper.

STIR-FRIED BEAN SPROUTS
AND RED PEPPER

PREP TIME: 2 MINUTES   **COOK TIME:** 5 MINUTES   **YIELD:** 2 SERVINGS

1 teaspoon sesame oil
1 cup (50 g) bean sprouts
⅓ cup (40 g) thinly sliced
   red pepper
Pinch salt
White pepper, to taste

Heat the oil in a medium skillet over medium heat. Add the sprouts and peppers, and stir-fry for a couple minutes. Season with the salt and pepper.

SALADS

GREEN BEANS AND TOMATO SALAD

PREP TIME: 5 MINUTES   **YIELD:** 2 SERVINGS

1 tablespoon (15 ml) rice vinegar
1 tablespoon (15 ml) vegetable oil
Pinch salt
Pinch sugar
Black pepper, to taste
¼ pound (113 g) green beans, trimmed and cut into 1½-inch (4 cm) pieces
5 cherry tomatoes, cut in half

1 In a small bowl, mix together the vinegar, oil, salt, sugar, and pepper.

2 Add the green beans and tomatoes, and toss to combine with the dressing.

TOMATO AND ONION SALAD

PREP TIME: 5 MINUTES   **YIELD:** 2 SERVINGS

2 medium tomatoes
¼ medium onion
1 teaspoon soy sauce
1 teaspoon freshly squeezed lemon juice
¼ teaspoon sugar
1 teaspoon sesame oil

1 Cut each tomato in half and then into 6 pieces. Slice the onion very thinly.

2 In a medium bowl, whisk together the soy sauce, lemon juice, sugar, and sesame oil. Add the tomatoes and onion, and combine.

SPINACH AND ARUGULA SALAD WITH LOTUS ROOT CHIPS

PREP TIME: 10 MINUTES   **COOK TIME:** 5 MINUTES   **YIELD:** 4 SERVINGS

1 small lotus root
2 cups (40 g) baby spinach
2 cups (40 g) baby arugula
1 tablespoon (15 ml) white vinegar
1 tablespoon (15 ml) extra-virgin
  olive oil
1 teaspoon honey
¼ teaspoon salt
Vegetable oil, for frying
8 cherry tomatoes, cut in half

1 Slice the lotus root into very thin slices (1 mm) with a mandoline. Remove excess moisture with paper towels and let dry for 10 minutes.

2 In a large bowl, combine the spinach and arugula. In a small bowl, whisk together the vinegar, olive oil, honey, and salt.

3 Heat 1 inch (2.5 cm) of vegetable oil in a large saucepan over medium-high heat (350°F, or 180°C). Add the lotus root slices and cook until crisp.

4 Just before serving, mix the greens with the dressing and top with the tomatoes and lotus chips.

POTATO SALAD

PREP TIME: 10 MINUTES   **COOK TIME:** 10 MINUTES   **YIELD:** 2 SERVINGS

1 medium russet potato, peeled and cut into 2-inch (5 cm) cubes

1 teaspoon vinegar

¼ teaspoon plus pinch salt, divided

1 Persian cucumber, thinly sliced

1 hard-boiled egg, chopped

1 tablespoon (14 g) mayonnaise

1 Boil the potato until soft, about 10 minutes. Drain and transfer to a medium bowl. Mash slightly with a fork and add the vinegar and ¼ teaspoon of the salt. Let cool.

2 In another medium bowl, sprinkle the cucumber with the remaining pinch of salt and let it sit for 2 to 3 minutes. Squeeze out excess water.

3 Add the cucumber, hard-boiled egg, and mayonnaise to the potato mixture and combine.

MACARONI SALAD

PREP TIME: 10 MINUTES   **COOK TIME:** 10 MINUTES   **YIELD:** 2 SERVINGS

½ cup (75 g) macaroni

1 small cucumber, thinly sliced

¼ medium carrot, cut into very thin matchsticks

Pinch salt, plus more to taste

1 slice ham, cut into thin strips

2 tablespoons (28 g) mayonnaise

Black pepper, to taste

1 Cook the macaroni according to the package directions. Drain and let cool.

2 Put the cucumber and carrot in a medium bowl, sprinkle with the pinch of salt, and let sit for 5 minutes until soft. Squeeze out excess water.

3 In another medium bowl, mix together the macaroni, cucumber, carrot, ham, and mayonnaise. Add salt and pepper to taste.

CARROT SALAD

PREP TIME: 5 MINUTES   **YIELD:** 2 SERVINGS

1 medium carrot
2 teaspoons rice vinegar
1 teaspoon vegetable oil
Pinch salt
Black pepper, to taste

1 Roughly shred the carrot using a vegetable peeler.

2 Mix with the remaining ingredients.

CAULIFLOWER AND SNOW PEA SALAD

PREP TIME: 2 MINUTES (PLUS 15 MINUTES CHILLING)   **COOK TIME:** 3 MINUTES   **YIELD:** 2 SERVINGS

1 cup (70 g) cauliflower florets
10 snow peas
½ teaspoon soy sauce
½ teaspoon mayonnaise
½ teaspoon vinegar
½ teaspoon vegetable oil
Pinch salt
Black pepper, to taste

1 Blanch the cauliflower and snow peas.

2 Put all ingredients in a bowl and mix. Refrigerate for 15 minutes or up to overnight.

BEAN SPROUTS AND BELL PEPPER NAMUL

PREP TIME: 2 MINUTES   **COOK TIME:** 2 MINUTES   **YIELD:** 2 SERVINGS

1 cup (50 g) bean sprouts
¼ medium green bell pepper, thinly sliced
2 teaspoons rice vinegar
1 teaspoon soy sauce
1 teaspoon sesame oil

1 Blanch the bean sprouts and bell pepper for 1 minute, drain, and transfer to a small bowl.

2 Add the vinegar, soy sauce, and sesame oil, and mix.

SHUNGIKU SALAD

PREP TIME: 5 MINUTES   **COOK TIME:** 1 MINUTE   **YIELD:** 2 SERVINGS

½ bunch shungiku (edible chrysanthemum leaves)
1½ teaspoons soy sauce
1½ teaspoons freshly squeezed lemon juice

1 Blanch the shungiku for 1 minute. Drain and cool under running water. Squeeze out excess water. Cut into 1-inch-long (2.5 cm) pieces.

2 In a medium bowl, mix together the soy sauce and lemon juice. Add the cooked shungiku and combine.

SNAP PEAS AND EGG SALAD

PREP TIME: 15 MINUTES   **COOK TIME:** 2 MINUTES   **YIELD:** 2 SERVINGS

1 large egg
12 snap peas
1 tablespoon (14 g) mayonnaise
¼ teaspoon freshly squeezed
   lemon juice
Pinch salt
Pinch white pepper

1 Hard-boil the egg and blanch the snap peas.

2 Coarsely chop the egg and cut the snap peas in half. Transfer to a medium bowl and combine with the mayonnaise, lemon juice, salt, and pepper.

COLESLAW AND ASIAN COLESLAW

PREP TIME: 5 MINUTES (PLUS 15 MINUTES CHILLING)   **YIELD:** 2 SERVINGS

COLESLAW
2 tablespoons (28 g) mayonnaise
1 tablespoon (15 ml) vinegar
2 teaspoons sugar
1 teaspoon vegetable oil
⅛ teaspoon salt
2 cups (140 g) shredded cabbage
¼ medium carrot, cut into very
   thin matchsticks

1 In a medium bowl, mix together the mayonnaise, vinegar, sugar, oil, and salt.

2 Add the cabbage and carrot, toss, and refrigerate for 15 minutes.

ASIAN COLESLAW
1½ tablespoons (23 ml) rice
   vinegar
1½ teaspoons sugar
1½ teaspoons sesame oil
⅛ teaspoon salt
2 cups (140 g) shredded cabbage
¼ carrot, cut into very thin
   matchsticks
1 green onion, chopped
¼ cup (15 g) chopped cilantro

1 In a medium bowl, combine the vinegar, sugar, sesame oil, and salt.

2 Add the rest of the ingredients, mix, and let it sit for at least 15 minutes.

SEAFOOD

OKAKA SNAP PEAS

PREP TIME: 5 MINUTES   **COOK TIME:** 7 MINUTES   **YIELD:** 2 SERVINGS

16 snap peas
1 tablespoon (0.75 g) crushed
  katsuobushi (dried bonito
  flakes)
¼ teaspoon soy sauce

1 Blanch the snap peas in salted water for 60 to 90 seconds. Drain and let cool for 1 minute. Cut them in half.

2 In a medium bowl, combine the peas, katsuobushi, and soy sauce.

OKAKA

PREP TIME: 1 MINUTE   **YIELD:** 2 SERVINGS

¼ cup (3 g) katsuobushi (dried
  bonito flakes)
½ teaspoon soy sauce

Mix together the katsuobushi and soy sauce.

OCTOPUS AND CUCUMBER SUNOMONO

PREP TIME: 10 MINUTES (PLUS 30 MINUTES CHILLING)   **YIELD:** 4 SERVINGS

½ teaspoon salt

2 Japanese or 4 Persian cucumbers, sliced into very thin rounds

3 tablespoons (45 ml) rice vinegar

1 tablespoon (15 ml) sugar

4 ounces (113 g) cooked sashimi-grade octopus, sliced into ¼-inch-thick (6 mm) pieces

1 In a medium bowl, stir the salt in with the cucumbers and let sit for 5 minutes. Squeeze out excess water.

2 In another medium bowl, mix together the rice vinegar and sugar until the sugar dissolves. Add the octopus and cucumbers to the vinegar mixture and combine. Chill in the refrigerator for 30 minutes before serving.

TUNA AND BROCCOLI SALAD

PREP TIME: 5 MINUTES   **COOK TIME:** 7 MINUTES   **YIELD:** 2 SERVINGS

1 cup (70 g) broccoli florets
1 to 2 tablespoons (10 to 20 g)
   tuna chunks (canned)
½ teaspoon soy sauce
1 tablespoon (14 g) Japanese
   mayonnaise
½ teaspoon ground sesame
   seeds

1 Blanch the broccoli florets for 1 minute. Drain and squeeze the moisture out of the tuna.

2 In a medium bowl, mix together the soy sauce, mayonnaise, and ground sesame seeds. Add the broccoli and tuna to the dressing and mix well.

TUNA AND POTATO NIMONO

PREP TIME: 5 MINUTES   **COOK TIME:** 30 MINUTES   **YIELD:** 2 SERVINGS

2 medium white potatoes
1 cup (235 ml) water
½ can (2.5 ounces, or 71 g) tuna,
   drained
1 tablespoon (15 ml) sugar
1½ tablespoons (23 ml) soy sauce
1 tablespoon (15 ml) sake
¼ cup (30 g) frozen green peas

1 Peel and cut the potatoes into 1-inch (2.5 cm) cubes.

2 Put the potatoes and water in a medium saucepan, cover, and cook over medium heat for about 10 minutes, or until tender. Add the drained tuna, sugar, soy sauce, and sake. Cook and stir, uncovered, for 10 minutes. Add the peas and cook for a couple minutes more. Cover and let cool.

MARINATED SHRIMP AND VEGETABLES

PREP TIME: 10 MINUTES (PLUS 1 HOUR OR UP TO OVERNIGHT MARINATING)   **COOK TIME:** 5 MINUTES
YIELD: 2 SERVINGS

6 to 8 shrimp, peeled and deveined

1 tablespoon (15 ml) extra-virgin olive oil

1 tablespoon (15 ml) freshly squeezed lemon juice

1 tablespoon (15 ml) apple cider vinegar (or vinegar of choice)

Pinch salt

Black pepper, to taste

¼ medium red bell pepper, cut in half crosswise and thinly sliced

4 snap peas

1 tablespoon (10 g) chopped red onion

1 teaspoon chopped fresh parsley

1 In a medium saucepan, boil the shrimp for 1 to 3 minutes, or until cooked. Drain and cool in ice water.

2 In a medium bowl, mix together the olive oil, lemon juice, vinegar, salt, and pepper. Add the cooked shrimp, bell pepper, snap peas, onion, and parsley, and marinate in the refrigerator for 1 hour or up to overnight.

POPCORN SHRIMP

PREP TIME: 10 MINUTES   **COOK TIME:** 5 MINUTES   **YIELD:** 2 SERVINGS

Vegetable oil, for frying
10 small shrimp, peeled and
   deveined
Salt and white pepper, to taste
2 tablespoons (30 ml)
   all-purpose flour
1 large egg, beaten
½ cup (25 g) bread crumbs
   (preferably panko)

1 In a medium skillet, heat the oil to 350ºF (180ºC) over medium-high heat. Carefully pat the shrimp dry with paper towels, making sure to remove any moisture. Sprinkle the shrimp with salt and pepper.

2 Lightly coat the shrimp in the flour, dip in the egg, and dredge in the bread crumbs.

3 Fry the shrimp until golden brown and the shrimp float in the oil, 2 to 3 minutes, turning once or twice. Set the shrimp on a cooling rack for a minute.

KOMBU TSUKUDANI (SEASONED SEA KELP)

PREP TIME: 15 MINUTES   **COOK TIME:** 25 MINUTES   **YIELD:** 2 SERVINGS

4 × 6-inch (10 × 15 cm) piece
   dried kombu (dried sea kelp)
½ cup (120 ml) water
½ teaspoon rice vinegar
1 tablespoon (15 ml) sugar
3 tablespoons (45 ml) soy sauce
1 tablespoon (15 ml) sake
1 tablespoon (15 ml) mirin
1 teaspoon sesame seeds

1 Place the kombu in a large bowl and add enough water to cover. Let sit for 15 minutes to rehydrate.

2 When the kombu becomes pliable, remove from the water, and pat dry. Slice thinly into 2-inch-long (5 cm) strips.

3 In a small saucepan, mix together the kombu, ½ cup (120 ml) water, and vinegar. Cook over medium-low heat for 10 minutes, then add the sugar, soy sauce, sake, and mirin. Cook and stir until the liquid is almost evaporated. Add the sesame seeds and mix.

MUSHROOMS

SAUTÉED SHIMEJI MUSHROOMS WITH SOY BUTTER SAUCE

PREP TIME: 2 MINUTES   **COOK TIME:** 3 MINUTES   **YIELD:** 2 SERVINGS

1 package (3.5 ounces, or 100 g) shimeji mushrooms
½ teaspoon vegetable oil
1 teaspoon butter
1 teaspoon sake
1 teaspoon soy sauce
½ green onion, chopped
Salt and white pepper, to taste

1 Trim the bottom of the mushrooms and separate into small pieces.

2 Heat the oil in a medium skillet over medium-high heat. Add the mushrooms and cook and stir for a couple minutes until softened. Add the butter, sake, soy sauce, and green onion, and stir. Add salt and pepper to taste if needed. Remove from the heat.

SAUTÉED MUSHROOMS AND ASPARAGUS

PREP TIME: 5 MINUTES   **COOK TIME:** 5 MINUTES   **YIELD:** 2 SERVINGS

5 ounces (140 g) asparagus
1 teaspoon vegetable oil
½ clove garlic, minced
6 cremini mushrooms, sliced
Pinch salt
Black pepper, to taste

1 Trim off the woody ends of the asparagus and cut each spear into 2-inch-long (5 cm) pieces.

2 Heat the oil and garlic in a medium skillet over medium heat. Add the asparagus and cook for 1 minute. Add the mushroom slices and cook for a few more minutes, until the vegetables are tender. Season with the salt and pepper.

SWEET AND SALTY SHIITAKE MUSHROOMS

PREP TIME: 2 MINUTES   **COOK TIME:** 10 MINUTES   **YIELD:** 2 SERVINGS

5 to 6 medium shiitake
    mushrooms, stems removed
    and caps thinly sliced
1 tablespoon (15 ml) sugar
1 tablespoon (15 ml) soy sauce
3 tablespoons (45 ml) water

1 Combine all the ingredients in a small saucepan.

2 Cover and cook over medium-low heat for 5 minutes, stirring occasionally.

3 Remove the lid and continue cooking until the liquid has evaporated.

BACON ROLL-UP WITH ENOKI MUSHROOMS

PREP TIME: 3 MINUTES   **COOK TIME:** 7 MINUTES   **YIELD:** 2 SERVINGS

½ package (3.5 ounces, or 100 g)
   enoki mushrooms
4 slices turkey bacon
½ teaspoon vegetable oil

1 Trim the bottom off the mushrooms and separate into 4 bunches.

2 Place 1 bunch on the end of a slice of bacon and roll up. Repeat with the remaining bunches and bacon.

3 Heat the oil in a large skillet over medium heat. Place the bacon rolls in the pan (end of the bacon strip down) and cook. Brown the bacon on all sides, turning frequently.

SIMMERED KOYA TOFU AND SHIITAKE MUSHROOMS

PREP TIME: 15 MINUTES (PLUS 2 TO 3 HOURS FOR SOAKING SHIITAKES)   **COOK TIME:** 25 MINUTES
YIELD: 4 SERVINGS

4 to 8 dried shiitake mushrooms

4 koya tofu (freeze-dried tofu; also spelled "koya-dofu")

2 cups (475 ml) Dashi (page XX)

3 tablespoons (38 g) sugar

2 tablespoons (30 ml) sake

2 tablespoons (30 ml) soy sauce

1 tablespoon (15 ml) mirin

1 Rehydrate the dried shiitake mushrooms in water for 2 to 3 hours, or until soft. Strain and reserve ¼ cup (60 ml) of the soaking water for later as it is packed with umami. Cut the mushrooms in half if too large.

2 Soak the koya tofu in plenty of water for 10 minutes. Squeeze out excess water and cut each tofu piece into quarters.

3 In a large saucepan, add the dashi, reserved mushrooms soaking water, sugar, sake, soy sauce, and mirin. Bring to a boil, then add the rehydrated shiitake and koya tofu. Reduce the heat and simmer for 20 minutes. Let cool in the pot.

SAUTÉED SHIITAKE MUSHROOMS

PREP TIME: 1 MINUTE   **COOK TIME:** 5 MINUTES   **YIELD:** 2 SERVINGS

1 teaspoon vegetable oil

4 to 6 shiitake mushrooms, stems removed and caps halved if needed

½ teaspoon soy sauce

1 Heat the oil in a medium skillet over medium-high heat. Add the mushrooms and cook on both sides until lightly browned and the moisture has evaporated.

2 Add the soy sauce and remove from the heat.

MARINATED MUSHROOMS

PREP TIME: 5 MINUTES (PLUS 1 HOUR OR UP TO OVERNIGHT MARINATING)   **COOK TIME:** 5 MINUTES
YIELD: 2 SERVINGS

1 package (5 ounces, or 140 g) enoki mushrooms

1 package (3.5 ounces, or 100 g) shimeji mushrooms

4 shiitake mushrooms

2 tablespoons (30 ml) extra-virgin olive oil

1 clove garlic, minced

1 dried red chile pepper, seeded and chopped (optional)

2 tablespoons (30 ml) apple cider vinegar (or vinegar of choice)

½ teaspoon salt

Black pepper, to taste

1 tablespoon (4 g) chopped fresh parsley

1 Trim the bottom off the enoki and shimeji mushrooms and separate into small pieces. Remove the shiitake stems and thinly slice the shiitake caps.

2 Heat the oil in a large skillet over medium-high heat. Add the garlic and chile pepper (if using), and cook and stir for 1 minute. Add the mushrooms and cook and stir for a few additional minutes, until softened.

3 Transfer the mushroom mixture to a medium bowl and add the vinegar, salt, and pepper. Let cool and add the parsley. Refrigerate for 1 hour or up to overnight.

EGGS AND MEAT

MISO BAKED CHICKEN

PREP TIME: 5 MINUTES (PLUS 3 HOURS OR UP TO OVERNIGHT MARINATING)   **COOK TIME:** 30 MINUTES
YIELD: 4 SERVINGS

¼ cup (64 g) miso paste
3 tablespoons (45 ml) mirin
2 tablespoons (30 ml) sake
1 tablespoon (15 ml) sugar
1 tablespoon (15 ml) soy sauce
4 boneless chicken thighs
Vegetable oil, for greasing

1 In a large bowl, mix together the miso, mirin, sake, sugar, and soy sauce. Mix in the chicken thighs and marinate in the refrigerator for at least 3 hours or up to overnight.

2 Preheat the oven to 425ºF (220ºC). Line a baking sheet with aluminum foil and grease with oil. Wipe off excess marinade from the chicken and place the chicken on the prepared baking sheet.

3 Bake the chicken for 15 minutes. Flip the chicken and bake for an additional 10 to 15 minutes, or until cooked through.

KINSHI TAMAGO (SHREDDED EGG CREPE)

PREP TIME: 5 MINUTES   **COOK TIME:** 5 MINUTES   **YIELD:** 2 SERVINGS

2 large eggs
Pinch salt
Vegetable oil, for cooking

1 Beat the eggs well with the salt.

2 Heat a small skillet over medium heat and coat with a thin layer of oil.

3 Pour some of the egg mixture into the pan, swirl the pan to spread it thin to make a thin egg sheet, and cook for 15 to 30 seconds. Flip it over, then immediately remove from the pan. Repeat this step until the egg mixture is gone. You should have 5 to 6 egg crepes.

4 Stack the crepes, roll them up, and cut them into ⅛-inch (3 mm) strips.

AVOCADO AND CHICKEN SALAD

PREP TIME: 5 MINUTES   **YIELD:** 2 SERVINGS

½ avocado

1½ teaspoons soy sauce

½ teaspoon sugar

½ teaspoon rice vinegar

½ cup (55 g) diced cooked
   (rotisserie) chicken

1 tablespoon (4 g) chopped
   fresh cilantro

1 Dice the avocado into ½-inch (13 mm) cubes.

2 In a medium bowl, combine the soy sauce, sugar, and rice vinegar.
   Add the avocado, chicken, and cilantro, and mix.

TAKO (OCTOPUS) SAUSAGE

PREP TIME: 3 MINUTES   **COOK TIME:** 5 MINUTES   **YIELD:** 2 SERVINGS

8 mini sausages
½ teaspoon vegetable oil
Ketchup or sauce of choice
  (optional)

1 Lay the sausage flat on the cutting board and cut one end lengthwise up to the middle. Rotate 90 degrees and cut again. This will make 4 legs. You can stop here or cut each leg into half to make 8 legs.

2 Heat the oil in a small skillet over medium heat. Cook and stir the sausages for 5 minutes.

3 If using, add the ketchup before turning off the heat.

HAM-WRAPPED ASPARAGUS

PREP TIME: 10 MINUTES   **COOK TIME:** 5 MINUTES   **YIELD:** 2 SERVINGS

4 to 8 spears asparagus, blanched
2 to 4 slices ham
½ teaspoon vegetable oil
Salt and black pepper, to taste

1 Trim off the woody ends of the asparagus and cut each spear crosswise into 3 pieces.

2 Cut the ham in half or just large enough to wrap a few pieces of asparagus. Wrap the asparagus with the ham.

3 Heat the oil in a medium skillet over medium heat. Add the ham-wrapped asparagus. Cook for 2 to 3 minutes per side. Sprinkle with salt and pepper to taste.

SAUTÉED GREEN PEAS AND SAUSAGE

PREP TIME: 2 MINUTES   **COOK TIME:** 8 MINUTES   **YIELD:** 2 SERVINGS

½ teaspoon vegetable oil
½ medium onion, finely chopped
6 to 10 mini sausages
½ cup (65 g) frozen peas
1 tablespoon (15 g) butter
Pinch salt
Black pepper, to taste

1 Heat the oil in a small skillet over medium-high heat. Add the onion and cook and stir until soft, 3 to 4 minutes.

2 Add the mini sausages and green peas, and cook for 4 to 5 minutes, or until heated through. Add the butter and stir until melted. Season with the salt and pepper.

PICKLED

CUCUMBER AND RADISH SUNOMONO

PREP TIME: 10 MINUTES   **YIELD:** 2 SERVINGS

2 Persian cucumbers, 1 to
    2 Japanese cucumbers,
    or ⅓ English cucumber
2 radishes
¼ teaspoon salt
1 tablespoon (15 ml) rice vinegar
1 teaspoon sugar
Dash soy sauce
½ teaspoon sesame seeds

1 Slice the cucumbers and radishes as thinly as you can and
  place in a small bowl. Stir in the salt and let sit for 5 minutes.
  Squeeze out the excess water.

2 In another small bowl, mix together the rice vinegar, sugar,
  and soy sauce until the sugar dissolves.

3 Add the vinegar mixture and sesame seeds to the prepared
  cucumbers and radishes, and mix well.

PICKLED DAIKON RADISH

PREP TIME: 10 MINUTES (PLUS 2 HOURS FOR RELEASING WATER AND MARINATING)   **YIELD:** 2 SERVINGS

½ pound (227 g) daikon radish

1 teaspoon salt, divided

1½ tablespoons (23 ml) rice vinegar

1½ teaspoons sugar

1 Peel the daikon and cut it into 2 × ½-inch-thick (5 cm × 13 mm) sticks. Put in a medium bowl and coat with ½ teaspoon of the salt. Let sit for 1 hour to release the water.

2 In another medium bowl, mix together the remaining ½ teaspoon salt, vinegar, and sugar. Lightly squeeze the water out of the daikon and toss with the vinegar mixture.

3 Cover and refrigerate for 1 hour.

DAIKON AND LEMON NAMASU

PREP TIME: 10 MINUTES (PLUS 30 MINUTES CHILLING)   **YIELD:** 2 SERVINGS

½ pound (227 g) daikon radish

¼ teaspoon salt

1½ tablespoons (23 ml) freshly squeezed lemon juice

1½ tablespoons (23 ml) rice vinegar

1 tablespoon (15 ml) sugar

1 to 2 teaspoons very thinly sliced lemon peel

1 Very thinly slice the daikon radish into 2-inch-long (5 cm) pieces. Sprinkle with the salt and let sit for 5 minutes. Squeeze out the excess water.

2 In a medium bowl, combine the lemon juice, vinegar, and sugar, and mix until the sugar is dissolved. Add the daikon and toss. Refrigerate for at least 30 minutes. Garnish with the lemon peel.

PICKLED BELL PEPPER

PREP TIME: 5 MINUTES   **COOK TIME:** 1 MINUTE   **YIELD:** 2 SERVINGS

1 tablespoon (15 ml) rice vinegar
1½ teaspoons sugar
Pinch salt
½ takanotsume (dried red
    chile pod), seeded and sliced
    (optional)
½ medium red or yellow bell
    pepper, cut into small wedges

1 In a small microwave-safe bowl, mix together the vinegar, sugar, salt, and red chile (if using). Toss the bell pepper in the vinegar mixture.

2 Microwave for 30 seconds, stir, and heat for 15 seconds more. Let cool.

CELERY SUNOMONO

PREP TIME: 8 MINUTES (PLUS 30 MINUTES CHILLING)   **YIELD:** 2 SERVINGS

2 celery ribs, very thinly sliced
¼ teaspoon salt
1 tablespoon (15 ml) rice vinegar
1 teaspoon sugar

1 In a small bowl, mix the celery with the salt and let sit for 5 minutes. Squeeze out the excess water.

2 In another small bowl, mix together the rice vinegar and sugar until the sugar dissolves. Add the vinegar mixture to the celery and mix well. If time permits, chill for 30 minutes before serving.

CUCUMBER AND SEAWEED SUNOMONO

PREP TIME: 15 MINUTES (PLUS 30 MINUTES CHILLING)   **YIELD:** 2 SERVINGS

1½ teaspoons dried wakame seaweed (¼ cup, or 20 g, rehydrated)
1 Japanese cucumber or 2 Persian cucumbers
¼ teaspoon salt
1 tablespoon (15 ml) rice vinegar
1 teaspoon sugar

1 In a medium bowl, rehydrate the wakame seaweed in water for 10 minutes. Squeeze out the excess water.

2 Slice the cucumber into very thin rounds, cutting as thinly as you can. Sprinkle the cucumber with salt and toss. Let sit for 5 minutes. Squeeze out the excess water.

3 In another medium bowl, mix together the vinegar and sugar. Add the seaweed and cucumber and mix well. If time permits, refrigerate for 30 minutes before serving.

SAUCES, DIPS, AND MORE

HUMMUS

PREP TIME: 5 MINUTES   **YIELD:** 2 SERVINGS

1 can (15 ounces, or 420 g)
   chickpeas, drained, or 1½ cups
   (340 g) well-cooked chickpeas
¼ cup (60 g) tahini
¼ cup (60 ml) extra-virgin olive oil
1 clove garlic, minced
2 tablespoons (30 ml) freshly
   squeezed lemon juice
½ teaspoon salt

Process all the ingredients in a food processor until smooth.

MENTSUYU (MULTIPURPOSE SAUCE)

PREP TIME: 2 MINUTES   **COOK TIME:** 10 MINUTES   **YIELD:** 2 SERVINGS

½ cup (120 ml) soy sauce
½ cup (120 ml) mirin
¼ cup (60 ml) sake
1 handful katsuobushi (dried
   bonito flakes)

1 In a small saucepan, bring all the ingredients to a boil, then remove from the heat.

2 Cool completely in the saucepan. Strain.

MISO WALNUTS

PREP TIME: 2 MINUTES   **COOK TIME:** 10 MINUTES   **YIELD:** 4 SERVINGS

4 ounces (113 g) walnuts
3 tablespoons (48 g) miso paste
3 tablespoons (45 ml) mirin
1 tablespoon (15 ml) sake
1 tablespoon (15 ml) sugar
Sesame seeds, for garnish

1 Dry-roast the walnut pieces in a medium skillet over medium-low heat until slightly browned.

2 In a medium saucepan, cook the miso, mirin, sake, and sugar over medium-low heat for 1 minute. Add the walnuts and coat with the sauce. Remove from the heat. Top with the sesame seeds.

FRESH FRUITS JELLY

PREP TIME: 10 MINUTES (PLUS 2 HOURS OR UP TO OVERNIGHT CHILLING)   **COOK TIME:** 3 MINUTES

YIELD: 2 SERVINGS

1 teaspoon powdered gelatin

½ cup (120 ml) plus 1 tablespoon (15 ml) white grape juice, divided

½ cup (65 to 75 g) fresh fruits* (such as halved grapes, chopped apples, oranges, melons, and berries)

* Avoid fruits that don't allow gelatin to set, such as pineapple, kiwi, and mango.

1 Mix the powdered gelatin with the 1 tablespoon (15 ml) of grape juice and let stand for 5 minutes.

2 Heat the remaining ½ cup (120 ml) grape juice in a small saucepan and turn off the heat before it comes to a boil. Add the gelatin and fruits, and mix.

3 Divide the liquid and fruits into individual cups with lids (such as yogurt containers) and refrigerate until firm, at least 2 hours or up to overnight.

STEWED APPLE

PREP TIME: 2 MINUTES   **COOK TIME:** 3 MINUTES   **YIELD:** 2 SERVINGS

1 large apple (such as Jonagold, Honeycrisp, or Fuji), cored and chopped

1 tablespoon (20 g) honey

1 teaspoon freshly squeezed lemon juice

In a microwave-safe bowl, toss the chopped apple, honey, and lemon juice. Cover and microwave for 3 minutes.

INDEX

ACKNOWLEDGMENTS

It all started with our website, Japanese Cooking 101, along with posting YouTube videos. If there were no fans and viewers for them, then we wouldn't be here writing this. You are a big part of our motivation and have kept us going forward. Thank you, everyone!

We appreciate Jeannine Dillon and her team from Race Point Publishing for giving us a "small" opportunity to publish OUR OWN cookbook! It is almost a miracle, we think, that they found us among hundreds of great cooks out there. Thank you, guys, very much for helping guide us through the process of putting our first book together.

Last but not least, to our families: our moms, who taught us how to show our affection through cooking, and our husbands and kids, who became our patient taste testers and endured eating cold bento for dinner for months—we love you all so much!

(And cheers to ourselves, for being actively there for each other for the last decade. That's pretty amazing!)